Fairy Haunts of Ireland

- a guide to magical, uplifting and supernatural sites for accessing the ancient spiritual heritage of Ireland and participating in her ever-luminous Other-world continuum.

by Alanna Moore

Alanna Moore is the author of:

Divining Earth Spirit - 1994, 2nd ed. 2004
Backyard Poultry – Naturally - 1998, 3rd ed. 2014
Stone Age Farming - 2001, 2nd ed. 2013
The Wisdom of Water - 2007
Water Spirits of the World - 2008, 2nd ed. 2012
Sensitive Permaculture - 2009
Touchstones for Today - 2013
Plant Spirit Gardener - 2016
Peasant in Paradise - 2021

Fairy Haunts of Ireland
by Alanna Moore

ISBN - 978-0-6452854-3-7

Published by Python Press
Australia & Ireland
Email - info@pythonpress.com.

© Text, photos and design by Alanna Moore 2023.

Illustrations on page 5 by Alanna Moore; pages 25, 59 & 71 and the cover by David Gascoigne; page 56 by Alice Khuan. Photos on page 6 by Andrea Donnoli; page 54 by Alice Khuan; pages 78 & 104 by Peter Cowman; and page 125 by Suzy Keys.

With thanks for editing help to Suzy Keys. Much gratitude to Ireland's fairy kingdoms and the lovely landscapes of the Irish shee.

All rights reserved. No part of this publication may be used or reproduced, apart from brief quotations, without written permission of the publisher.

Cover: 'Legendary Leitrim', by David Gascoigne, 2014.

Table of Contents

Introduction   5

How the Australian author, a professional geomancer practising for over 40 years, developed understanding and connection to Irish spirits of place via Aboriginal Dreaming.

Chapter 1 Who, what and where are the fairies?   7

Fairy stories - 8. What species of sí can be found? - 9. Nature spirits and human spirits - 11. The Banshee - 12. Fairy Passes - 13. Fairy Forts - 14. Visiting Holy Fairy Places -16. Appreciating Otherworldly sites -17.

Chapter 2 Irish goddesses and gods   19

Brigid - 20. From Neolithic and Indian to Iron Age deities - 21. The Cailleach and the Crane cult - 24. Gods of light and darkness - 28. Crom Dubh - 29.

Chapter 3 Finding the Fairies.   35

Fairy places to visit in Co Sligo - 35. Leitrim - 37. Tipperary - 39. Wicklow - 39. Finding Fairy Passes in Co.s Leitrim/Cavan/Fermanagh - 40. Seven Years in a Fairyfield - 42.

Chapter 4 Finding Water Spirits   47

Mannanán mac Lir - 48. Holy rivers - 48. Meeting a river goddess - 49. Water fairy places to visit in Northern Ireland - 52. In Co.s Carlow & Wexford - 52. Kildare - 52. Roscommon - 53. Cavan - 55. Sligo -57. Donegal - 58. Fermanagh - 58. Monaghan - 59. Cork - 60.

Chapter 5 Finding Sun Goddesses   63

Visiting the homes of goddesses & fairy queens in Co. Limerick - 63. Kerry - 65. Cork - 66. Tipperary - 67. Tyrone - 68. Armagh - 69. Westmeath -70. Galway - 70. Roscommon - 71. Longford - 72. Offaly -73

Chapter 6 Finding Mountain Gods
& Heroes of the Divine Masculine   75

Visiting their homes in Co. Limerick - 75. Fermanagh - 77. Kildare - 78. Mayo - 78. Longford - 79. Clare - 80. Cork - 80. Kerry - 81. Antrim - 82. Westmeath - 83. Sligo 83. Dancing with the Daghda - 83.

Chapter 7 Finding the Sacred Cow   85

Sacred cow places across Co. Donegal - 86. Meath & Kildare - 86. Leitrim - 88. Sligo - 90. Longford - 90. Clare - 90. Galway - 91.

Chapter 8 Finding the Cailleach   93

The divine hag in Co. Meath - 94. Journey to the Underworld - 96. In Longford - 100. Armagh -100. Sligo - 100. Galway - 102. Mayo - 102. Cork - 104. Donegal - 105. Roscommon - 106. Derry - 106. Clare - 106. Kerry - 107. Legacy of the crone - 107.

References   109

Index   115

Resources   121

Introduction

This is a book inspired by a lifetime of experiences of the fairy world across Australia and Ireland. It also draws upon the observations, experiences and theories of others who've likewise encountered or become curious about the Other - the subtle, intelligent dimensions of the spiritual reality of life.

Growing up in Australia and unburdened by a mainstream religious view, I found my own way of thinking that was informed by indigenous perspectives. My first school in the early 1960s was with Aboriginal kids and we'd dig up edible roots in the playground for snacks. Later I met Aboriginal elders and learnt about the Dreaming of their Country*, of the spirit beings who were there from the beginning, creating landscapes and continuing to reside in the land, their sacred site homes officially recognised and protected by federal laws, in theory at least.

Clairvoyantly sensing the spirits of place helped to reinforce these understandings. I spent time with people who could see them clearly and gained confidence in my own impressions. Becoming a professional geomancer, advising people about subtle energies and spirit beings in the environment, I realised that animistic perspectives were once universal. It's our common cultural base. Animism's demise ushered in the exploitation of nature and Country everywhere.

From teaching the art of dowsing in the early 1980's, helping people develop their innate intuition and sense of subtle energies, I started to share techniques to locate and connect with nature spirits. These beings can be found by anyone who learns to dowse. You don't have to be especially 'gifted', just open and curious.

They can be detected by dowsing their basic form - as spherical energy fields that move around and expand and contract at will. I was a presenter at the British Society of Dowsers international conference in 2003, that had a theme of 'New Work', and I introduced this new subject to them. It's been so rewarding to share this and I still find it a vast and exciting field of discovery.

But Aboriginal Dreaming is not my ancestral heritage. There are limits to my connection to it and I'm not qualified to know or talk of its secrets. So much has been taken from indigenous Australians in the brutal course of colonisation and often all they have left are stories, their greatest cultural treasures. I can only speak of my own experiences.

Having both English and Irish ancestry, I always felt at home in Ireland and I live there now. On a recent sojourn to Australia, before returning home I chatted to an Aboriginal woman elder who spoke passionately about concerns for her Country in north central Victoria. I was proud to tell her -

"*I'm going back to my Dreaming Country now*".

And so I came back to Ireland in March 2023 and started to finish writing this book. I hope it inspires you to connect into the Other-dimensional worlds, the spiritual realities of the island of Ireland. Or anywhere.

Alanna Moore dowsing at a sacred stone in Italy, Oct. 2023. Photo - A Donnoli

* "*For First Nations people, your identity is totally related to Country, your own Country where your particular clan comes from,*" says Margo Ngawa Neale, senior Indigenous art and history curator at the National Museum of Australia. "*We spell it with a capital C because it is not country as with Israel or America — it is not a surface thing, it is not cartographic. We see Country as a personage, as a living being. It holds the wisdom and knowledge and all the features are the result of the ancestral beings who have travelled the country and created it.*"

Source - https://www.abc.net.au/news/2023-10-04/significance-connection-to-country-songlines-indigenous-culture/102925228

Chapter One
Who, what and where are the fairies?

Like all people, the Irish were originally animists, aware that consciousness is inherent in all nature. They had a deep knowing of the land and the intangible realms that co-exist with ours. They respected the parallel world of nature spirits, the genius loci in landscapes, and they sought to live in harmony with them.

So just who and what are fairies? This is more a question of - to whom did the Irish relate to amongst the many species in 'fairyland'? For fairies, when we use the word in a generic manner, come in a vast array of shapes and sizes, with many names and attributes, functions and activities. Fairy beings exist on multi-dimensional levels of frequency, typically in what the Theosophists, ancient wisdom seekers from the late 19th century, would call the etheric and astral planes of life. A characteristic of astral matter is its ability to create any desired visual form, for seers to recognise the beings. That's why we tend to read reports of a characteristic look to them; they might always appear garbed in medieval clothing, for example.

Human animals can be described as multi-dimensional fields of intelligent energy, our energetic entities constituting a species of nature spirit that's also embodied with a physical field. Today's theorem of quantum physics can accommodate the Other-world. German quantum physicist Berkhard Heim's model of twelve dimensions of reality, for example, would place fairies on the fifth and sixth dimensional levels.[1]

Fairy beings have varying degrees of consciousness and intelligence. They develop and evolve over time, as we do, and also influence the evolution of plant and animal forms. Such 'intelligent design' makes much more sense than Darwin's idea of random mutations to be the driver of evolution. (His peer Lamarck had a better grasp of the organic evolutionary process.) Generally speaking, the smaller, less evolved species have less intelligence than the larger ones and their lives are far simpler. Tiny flower fairies, whose job it is to open and care for blossoms only, for example. We'll not be focussing on such ubiquitous beings. Rather, we'll look at the larger, more evolved and intelligent species in the landscape. These are the ones that Irish fairy stories refer to and that we're encouraged to navigate carefully to keep in their good books. They are a force for connectivity and protective care, their higher intelligence informing beings concerned with evolution (plant devas, etc) about what adaptations are needed and when.

Fairy lore in Ireland has ancient roots. Many Irish people are descendants of the indigenous cruithin, the earliest peoples. They arrived after the 2km deep ice sheets of the Ice Age had melted away, some 14,000 years ago. Archeological analysis of Bear bones butchered by hunters dates them to around 10,500 BC, making this the earliest Human record found here. As author Manchan Magan puts it,

"We've been working the same land and speaking the same language for thousands of years. The continuity of tradition and lore is more like the Aboriginals in Australia than anything you'll find elsewhere in Europe." [2]

Familiarity with place is so strong here. Some place names are a couple of thousand years old and the whereabouts of fairy haunts is well established, often immortalised in place names. Indeed, much of the Irish language is imbued with fairy words and concepts, showing the cultural importance fairies once held. Unfortunately for Northern Ireland, much of the continuity of place tradition was broken when British invaders took up the most fertile lands and cruelly ejected the cruithin owners.

It's convenient to use the term fairy, or better still the Irish word sí, or sidhe, pronounced shee, as a shorthand for the multitude of beings. The sí, however, is a term never used in their presence. They were instead diplomatically referred to as the Good People, the Gentry, the Little People and the like. Unlike sugar-sweet depictions of wish-fulfilling Victorian era British fairies, the Irish sí are a force to be reckoned with, especially if upset by destructive human activities.

Fairy stories

So, how have the sí been described and what are the best sources of information about them? I'm not the first to say that official sources are less to be trusted than local folklore. While there's a wealth of literary traditions from medieval times, these can mainly be classed as either pseudo-historical, fantasy or spin-doctoring. Consider the context and reason why they were written. Medieval monk writers were hostile to fairy beings and aimed to downplay their influence and demonise them. Images from Victorian era British fairy tales (such as overleaf) are romanticised visions of sugary sweet quality for wholesome children's books. Real fairies don't need wings and don't go around granting wishes at the drop of a hat - you have to earn their respect first!

Eye witness accounts of fairies in stories collected by the likes of authors W. Y. Evans-Wentz and Nobel prize winner W. B. Yeats, who heard them from neighbours during his childhood, are more grounded in the spiritual reality. However, the fairy stories told to Lady Gregory, an eager collector in Co. Galway, can't be so well trusted. While she was well meaning and even learned to speak Irish, her husband was a politician involved with legislation designed to further oppress the peasantry. The locals found an interesting way to retaliate through her. Lady Gregory was said to have

"*gathered material for her books and plays in the cabins and cottages of Clare-Galway, where she had been industriously plied with folklore specially invented for her visits, and all of which she had innocently accepted.*"
As well, she also translated the Saga of Cuchulain of Muirthemne around 1902, but, thinking that it "*might be used as a school book…meant that she took great care not to include material that would shock the prudish.*" [3]

During the 1930s a nation-wide project to preserve folk wisdom and stories, including tales of the Other-worlds, was undertaken by school children at the request of the Folklore Commission. They collected a treasure trove of material, often with more archaic elements than versions written by medieval monks. The collection has recently been designated as being of international importance by UNESCO, an honour only shared in Ireland with the much more famous Book of Kells.

What species of sí can be found?

A medieval classification system for nature spirits was described by Paracelsus, the Swiss physician and alchemist in the 16th century who assigned them, according to tradition, to the four elements. Elemental beings are either located in the earth (e.g. 'gnomes'), air ('sylphs'), fire ('salamanders') or waters ('undines'), he wrote.[4] The scheme is useful, but a bit restrictive. What about the elements of wood and metal, as in the Chinese scheme? Also, some beings change their elemental preferences, Australian Aboriginal lore has shown this, for example the Yawk Yawk spirit of the Top End that starts life underwater, but on maturing moves up onto the land to live there part time. So

Who, what and where are the fairies?

calling them elementals doesn't always do them justice. Sovereignty goddesses and gods are also highly mobile between their domains of land and water. Fairies can act like microcosms of these beings, presiding over smaller sized territories and, when threatened, defending their Dreaming Country as best they can - we invade or degrade it at our peril!

The types of sí one can find vary according to the types of environments they occupy, from farms to mountains, coastlines and forests, to homes and monuments. The Irish interacted more with certain types than with others. Evans-Wentz wrote in 1910 of a woman seer who told him about five main species she'd encountered in Ireland.[5] These five types, with comments by the author and others, are:

1. The Gnomes - these small beings live under the ground and are either indifferent or friendly to people. They can get grumpy or mischievous when their homes are disturbed, such as when, say, foundations are being sunk for a house. Their energy can be quite unpleasant to be around then.

2. Leprecauns and Cluricauns - are small, merry, frisky little beings. Cluricauns can attach to certain families and might live in the cellar of a house. Depictions of leprecauns sold in tacky Irish tourist shops, derived from images created by Walt Disney for the 1959 movie 'Darby O'Gill and the Little People' make many people cringe. However Disney was actually using the descriptions given in 375 eye-witness accounts contained in the Folklore Commission's Schools Manuscript Collection.[2]

3. The Little People - who are small and *"good looking"*. There are many varieties in different habitats across the island of Ireland. One species would be the little moon-faced, child-like beings I observed one full-Moon-lit evening in the wild mountains of north Leitrim.

4. The Good People - also known as the Gentry, Gentle Folk and People of Peace. As tall as people, these beautiful beings *"direct the magnetic currents of the Earth."* Their tribes are each ruled by a fairy queen and they prefer to live inside hills. (In other countries they might be called Elves.) In the past, these People of Peace were more war-like in the folklore. There are tales of fairy battles, where regional groups fought each other regularly. On the Human level this took the form of faction fighting, as there was a lot of tribal chauvinism going on. Fairies tend to emulate what they observe of human behaviour (while also mimicking our looks and clothing). With tribal hostilities largely over in Ireland now, the fairies have become more peaceful.

5. **Goddesses and gods** - the most highly evolved of nature beings, who can manifest anywhere and everywhere. They transcend time and space in their movements and enjoy interactions with Humans, who they co-develop with. Their fractal, individual manifestations can be found in many places. A sub-class perhaps, the Banshee are white female spirits associated with particular families and imminent death.

The seer woman added that *"there may be many other classes of invisible beings which I do not know"*.[5] But her list is certainly a good starting point. You'll notice there's no mention of 'evil spirits' that christians might expect. In forty years of consultancy work I've not often come across them, but I also don't look for them. Perhaps evil people or evil intentions attract, or even create them? However nature spirits can become demonised from trauma. From my experience, one can soothe and placate them, if open to gaining an understanding of their plight and perhaps helping to rectify the problem. Saying sorry on behalf of Humankind can go a long way too!

The seer woman also didn't mention giant forest spirits, such as ones I've encountered in forested parts of Europe. In Sweden these are called Trolls, in Poland, the Leshi (written about in my book 'Plant Spirit Gardener'[6].) This absence comes as no surprise because in 1910 Ireland had virtually no forests, certainly no old growth ones. Only 1% forest cover was left when the British departed, having been exploited for building ships used for warfare and to transport slaves and prisoners, plus the wealth extracted from colonies.

Nature spirits and Human spirits

It's interesting to consider why some Irish people felt that the sí were the spirits of dead people, as seers would sometimes recognise familiar faces in amongst fairy hordes. I think this idea is a slight confusion. Someone better informed told Evans-Wentz -
"When people died it was said the Gentry took them, for they would afterwards appear among the Gentry." [5] Others have it that only those who die prematurely are taken in by them, they have no interest in old folks. Such observations hold true today. One of my cherished seer informants, Billy Arnold, was similarly taken in by the sí in Australia after he died in 2012. (Another seer observed that this was the case and told his daughter.)

Who, what and where are the fairies?

When Aboriginal people are about to die, tradition expects them to go back to the land of their forebears so that their spirits can return to the sacred places from whence they originated. So it's not surprising that spirits of their dead sometimes manifest to white people living on the land. This is normal and one should never consider moving these spirits on 'to the light' - a dangerous concept from the New Age movement in that it doesn't consider different cultural expectations of death. Instead, it's better to show those spirits respect and leave them alone!

The pagan Irish were of a similar mind on this matter. For them, the spirits of the dead went to Tir Na Og, the Land of the Young, which happens to be all around us because it's the Other-dimensional world. Here the dead can be observed by seers as their youthful selves. Sometimes Tir na Og was said to be an island, or somewhere else, but this could be a misunderstanding and generally it was not thought to be so. The more modern concept of a pie-in-sky distant Heaven is merely a thought-form, to use a Theosophical term.

The Banshee

The Banshee, meaning fairy woman, is associated with particular clans and she is heard to howl eerily or sing before one of them dies. Sometimes considered a house fairy, Banshees are found across Ireland and are not so much associated with places as they are with families. Some are viewed as young, others as old women, but legends usually describe a small, older woman. Typically dressed in white, she tends to have long hair, either white or grey, that she combs while making her spine chilling calls. The keening of funeral attendant women is probably a tradition that stems from the Banshee's behaviour. Or perhaps the Banshee learned it from the women? The Irish have a strong culture of death and funeral practises going back to the times when megalithic mounds were erected to house the bones of ancestors and provide powerful statements of tribal identity and territoriality.

Some people in the past considered the Banshee to be a dead relative who was fondly attached to her family and kept close by, warning them of impending doom and death. W. B. Yeats wrote about a Banshee associated with his mother's family, the Pollexfens of Sligo. This being would manifest in the form of a white bird.[7] While not a place fairy as such, according to 19th century writer O'Hanlon the cries of the Banshee would often emanate from a spring, river or lake that's connected with her.[8] Considering this twist, it's starting to sound like the Banshee is a downgraded sovereignty goddess, who delivers ominous messages as She is associated with both life and death. And as once the great bird Goddess, She still travels in the guise of a white bird. But what message might be had from fairies in general? Magan sums it up nicely.

"Their message seems to be one of disattachment from human obsessions; we should instead follow their lead by dancing, feasting, and taking it easy." [2]

Fairy Passes

Fairies don't need wings to flit or glide around the place, they're not much affected by gravity. (They do have a certain amount of weight to them, however, and will sometimes perch on horizontal tree branches.) But they find it easy, though not essential, to travel along meandering Earth energy lines that the Irish called Fairy Passes or Fairy Paths (to the Chinese - Dragon Lines). These serpentine energy flows rise up from out of the ground in an upward vortex, meander along the contours of the land, and later earth themselves at a downward vortex point, such geo-vortices being sometimes called a Fairy Hole. The lines flow in a toroidal vortex form (think of smoke rings) and follow the laws of fluid dynamics. Not that there are any 'laws of nature', there are only human-made theories. However, the toroidal vortex is a useful model to understand how Fairy Passes move across the land.

If you can identify Fairy Passes, such as by dowsing for them, they can be followed and will no doubt lead you to special places. The Chinese would call this 'riding the dragon'. They're often found connecting a couple of 'fairy forts' together. This shows the pattern of traffic between their homes, that was once Human, then fairy. Any regular movement of beings along a particular pathway leaves a residual, dowse-able energy current that builds up over time. So, we can't say that the Fairy Passes were there first, they may simply be an artefact of fairy movements that's perceivable to the dowser and seer. Many an Irish fairy story warns of obstructing, or worse, building a home over a Fairy Pass, with the dire consequences to people who were unfortunate to be living *"in the way"* (the Galway term recorded by Lady Gregory). This concept still holds true, as I find in my professional work as a geomancer and 'fairy whisperer'. The following example being typical.

"They should never have built over that Fairy Pass," were words that kept echoing in my head as I recently map dowsed an Irish home that had been extended across one and was ever since having problems. There were 'bad vibes', thwarted endeavours, sleeplessness and all sorts of blockages, including

in the new sewerage system, some of which had to be replaced. An old Apple tree had been cut down too, so I wasn't at all surprised to find out what had been happening there, after initially discovering the obstructed Fairy Pass. (Fortunately, we were were able to re-direct the energy flow of the Fairy Pass, which improved things immensely.)

It's a perennial problem and the reason why, in the past, people cautiously staked out their building site somehow and waited to see if anything had been interfered with, as a sign of fairy disapproval. For example, some would place little piles of stones on the four corner positions and leave them overnight. Ideally they were still standing the next morning. As I say to clients, it's better to obtain 'planning permission from the fairies' in advance, before inadvertently upsetting them and invoking their wrath.

Fairy Forts

So-called fairy forts are landscape features with Other-worldly attributes. These circular walled homestead sites are very common in wilder farmland areas and are often found on hilltops, on a knoll, or rise in the ground. In Irish they were variously called a lios, liss, or rath. The 'forts' are a good example of how special sites evolve over time to become fairy places. Dating mostly from the Iron Age, some were still inhabited until the 17th century. Prior to that time, wolves were a big problem for farmers with livestock. So farm animals were corralled into them for safety at night. People made the raths by digging a circular bank and ditch, on top of which was planted prickly bushes, such as Blackthorn. In regions where stone was plentiful they might have used stones for the enclosure, although these usually represent a more affluent owner and are called in Irish cashels (castles). Biodegradable homes of wattle and daub (sticks and mud) were built inside the walls.

The English transcription - 'ring fort' - just means a place with defence against animal predators, rather than any military associations. Raths were not the best defence against marauding Humans. But in times of warfare, some raths were equipped with a hidden refuge - underground chambers and passages in which to hide, called souterrains by archeologists. These have been sometimes found with remnant lumps of butter in them and they did offer a cool place for food storage. Nevertheless, over the centuries the inhabitants were overrun in tribal wars and slaughtered in their homes, or they moved on and the raths were abandoned. But never forgotten.

Fairy Haunts of Ireland

Perhaps as the Traveller folk of Ireland might burn the caravan of a deceased person, so it may have been considered unlucky for the living to continue residing in the old raths that became known as places for the dead, with a taboo status. In the christian era it was once common for unbaptised children to be buried within raths, not being allowed on church grounds. I believe that one such rath is found near my home, for, according to a client, *"on some nights I hear the sounds of babies crying coming from the liss."*

The taboo to never disturb a rath and the plants growing on it has preserved the sites from disturbance. Legends warn about the consequences of gathering wood or removing stones, or anything from raths. Even to this day, people on the land will talk of the ill-effects of molesting them. So, the fairies have taken full advantage of this protected/neglected status because they prefer to be stationed in wild places where people won't interfere with their homes. Hence the modern appellation of 'fairy fort'.

Many raths are the fairies' domain now and it's best not to visit one unless you get their permission first! Folks visiting a rath or other special fairy place might first check in with them mentally and announce themselves; asking something like *"By your leave"*, as Paul Deveraux has noted.[9] Just as the Australian Aboriginals might call out or sing to a place first, to make their presence known.

Visiting Holy Fairy Places

People talk of visiting 'holy places'. What are they exactly? Rupert Sheldrake explains that *"holiness is about connection and relationship. The word comes from a root that means whole or healthy."* Sheldrake, an amazing biologist and a patron of the British Pilgrimage Trust, encourages us to pilgrimage to holy places. As an eloquent advocate for the concept of morphic resonance and morphogenetic fields that influence people and places, he suggests that

> *"...holy places may be holy because they contain a kind of memory of what has happened there before. ...When we enter a holy place we are exposed to the same stimuli as those who have been there before and therefore come into resonance with them. If pilgrims to a holy place have been inspired, uplifted and healed there, we are more likely to have similar experiences of spiritual connection. Holy places can grow in holiness through people's experiences within them."*[10]

People also talk about visiting 'power centres' in the landscape. The Irish have a different view again. They speak of 'gentle places', where the 'people of peace' are stationed and where the feeling of grace and magic is palpable. It is these places that are worth our while to seek out, where we can bathe in their essence; find where the good folk dance and make their revelries, and where we can dance too, even dance with them! These are the best of places for the nourishment and delight of our spirits.

Fairy places are not usually marked by special monuments, although they can be. Places of human sanctuary and repose do appeal to fairies, as do places of ritual and ceremony. But natural environments are much preferred. Special stones, water sources and waterbodies, wild waterfalls, old trees and groves, tangled gardens where the lawn mower does not rule supreme, and the like, are a natural choice of residence for fairy beings.

Every area has its fairy places. And, though some places are more magical than others, we can find them almost anywhere in natural environments. In this book I've chosen mostly well known, well-documented or stand out places to describe, and I've visited a few that I can pass personal comments on. But it's not an exhaustive list by any means. One needs to assess folklore in one's own area, and go and discover them for oneself in a suitable state of mind.

Appreciating Other-worldly sites

How to pilgrimage to Other-worldly places? Are there protocols? The continuum of spiritual practises long performed at sites is a good starting point. We can merge into this continuum, resonate with age-old sacred connections and harmonise with the morphogenetic field of place, as Sheldrake would see it.

Our journeys to special sites are all the better for being slow and intentional. Walking the paths, not rushing. Taking our time. Sheldrake suggests walking to them with a special pilgrim's staff of Hazel wood, or the like; and singing suitable songs or chants to the trees, stones, holy wells etc. I've observed the spirits of place mightily impressed by such actions!

Arriving at the site - don't just dive straight in. Meander. Announce yourself and your intentions, silently or out loud. Being sensitive and receptive, ask permission of the guardians of the site. Wait for a positive reply, be open to signals from the Other-world. Only when properly ready is it time to proceed.

Then walk around the site in a meditative state of mind. Traditionally this is done three times. *"This circumambulation...helps to make the holy place the centre,"* as Sheldrake puts it. Within the holy place, open yourself to the magic and mystery. Be in the now. Take note of first impressions. Here you can respectfully make your offerings, be it flowers or loving feelings. For, whether material (let it be biodegradable!) or intangible - there's no difference. Our offerings are *"personal expressions of grace and gratitude."* [11]

Here you can heartily sing songs, do toning or chanting. To make the experience really special and to harness the power of intention, it's best to use appropriate lyrics in a language we can understand. We can write our own song and chant lyrics, ones that are culturally appropriate to self and place. (My own song Singing to the Land was written for such occasions.[12])

At the holy place we might meditate and pray, ask the beings of place for their insights and blessings, and give them heartfelt thanks. In the Dreamtime state of mind, the possibility of the 'lifting of the veils' between our world and the Other is greatly heightened.

> I've found that the fairies are out there
> and they're eagerly waiting for us to do this!

Who, what and where are the fairies?

Chapter Two
Irish Goddesses and Gods

Just as we have many species of the sí, so there are also many types of deified beings. Deities are simply more highly evolved, glorified versions of nature spirits. The focussed energy of human veneration has vastly increased their size, power, intelligence and influence. Thus they've co-evolved with Human beings, in the process gaining Human-like attributes. I've observed this process of co-evolution myself on a small farm in Victoria, Australia. The female 'landscape angel' at an Aboriginal women's sacred site was at first shy and sleepy, virtually curled up in a ball. But over the fourteen years I spent there, with all my interactions with her, she became a tall, gorgeous to behold, powerfully active landscape being, who also acted as my totem (connected into my energy field).

Traditionally, the premier deities were simply referred to as 'the goddess/god of my tribe', while their more personal names were generally kept secret. Generic names often translate as 'the Mother' (e.g. in Greece - Demeter), or 'the Father' (e.g. Dispater, the Roman Underworld 'Rich Dad'). When invading tribes swept into Ireland they brought their own deities with them and these were accommodated into existing pantheons with differing levels of success. The endemic beings didn't go away, but had to jostle for position. A great deal of recycling, rape and hybridisation went on. Over time original legends were lost, fragmented, censored and deliberately altered to suit prevailing tastes and politics. The tales can be confusing to follow, plus many have elements plagiarised from other deities and cultures. And there are so many put-downs! Mud slinging replaces what remains of the noble memory of once highly regarded beings.

The early Irish church also re-cast many popular deities as saints and these became integrated into folk belief. Powerful goddesses were re-invented as positively pure saints. St Brigid, for example, was said to glow as a baby - probably as a result of a sunny goddess lineage. Imagery of the likes of continental Sun god Lugh may have also been borrowed by the church to become the bright light of Jesus and St Patrick, to contrast the earlier dark, chthonic gods.

Back in Neolithic times, from some 12,000 years ago, when hunter gathering was transformed by the advent of agriculture and more sedentary lifestyles,

Ireland's tribes were ruled by Great Mother triple goddesses who were passionately connected with territory and the fertility of the land. They worked with partner gods to care for and protect the tribes that revered them. Representing the sovereignty of the sacred land, there was a political dimension to them. Tribes sought to legitimise their rule, with kings symbolically marrying the prevailing goddesses of the land.

From around the fifth century BCE invading patriarchal Celtic tribes came to Ireland and Britain causing the demise of sovereignty goddesses, who were ravaged and usurped by the new incoming order of sky gods. Invaders killed the menfolk and married the women. They brought with them war goddesses such as the triple Morrígan, a goddess triad consisting of Badh, Macha and Anand/Morrígan[13], but these are not much remembered now. In Wales, the Mabinogion stories give insights into Celtic legacy and the transition from paganism to christianity. They *"document the descent of the Celtic goddess from her exalted position of lady sovereignty, great queen and mistress of the bards, to the ambiguous roles of fairy, wise woman and dreaded witch"*.[14] In Ireland it was the same and early spin-doctors gave Her a dressing down here too. So, original goddesses have morphed into many forms and disguises, and they continue to inspire us to this day!

Brigid

Transformed Irish goddesses linger on in folk memory and the ever popular St Brigid comes immediately to mind. Her persona is a continuum of goddess Brigid, a goddess often equated with the British Brigantia and Britannia, but not actually the same being. Author Brian Wright thinks that goddess Brigid was 'invented' by invading Celtic tribes around 2000 years ago, their Druids giving Her an appropriate native lineage, as being the daughter of the Daghda and the Morrigan.[15] Typically portrayed as a gentle maiden and protector of mothers and livestock, she was sometimes called the Bride of the Kine, and was often in the company of Cows or even became a Cow.[16] She follows in the footsteps of Indian goddess and culture bringer Lakshmi in being credited with the invention of writing, poetry, medicine and metalwork.

In her stronghold of Kildare, goddess Brigid had an Oak grove where priestesses tended a sacred fire that was never allowed to go out. The last chief Druidess of this temple may have become the real historical St Brigid. Eventually the sacred fire there was extinguished, but then in 1993 a perpetual fire was reinstated by the Brigidine Sisters.[15] Brigid's sacred day is Imbolc,

February 1st, the first day of spring and named for the first flush of milk in sheep. From 2023 St Brigid's Day is now a designated public holiday in Ireland. So She still holds currency today, despite being expunged from the official list of saints sanctioned by the Vatican in 1969.

The sacred purity remembered of Brigid made her an ideal candidate for transference to the early christian pantheon. Raunchier old goddesses could not be reconciled by the church so easily and were killed off in stories. During the Iron Age, goddess Maeve, the 'fairy queen of Connaught', was a king maker and the symbols expressing her divine sexuality were the comb and casket. In one story she gave these sacred objects to maiden goddess Erne, who was 'drowned' under the waters of newly formed Lough Erne.[16] (Why She did this in the enemy territory of Ulster is not explained, therefore implausible.) However it happened, Erne is no doubt merged as one with Her domain and continues to live there still as the presiding water spirit.

From Neolithic and Indian to Iron Age deities

The Great Goddess of Neolithic Ireland was triple in aspect, as maiden, mother and crone. An early sovereignty goddess who gave Her name to the country, Ériu was one of three, together with Banba and Fódla. Older again was Danu, or Anu/Ana, a pan-European mother goddess, who probably originated in India and was said to be the mother of the gods of the Tuatha Dé Danaan in Ireland. Another earlier name of this tribe was the Tuath Dé, tribe of the gods. The triple goddess had Her partners too, Ériu / Banba / Fódla being married to Mac Gréine, Mac Cuill and Mac Cécht.

The European Great Goddess and Her consorts are seen in a famous depiction on the silver panels of the Gundestrup Cauldron, a rare find dug up by turf cutters from a Danish bog and dated to the second century BCE. On its silver panels we see Her sacred roles throughout the year; Her prominent size in contrast to smaller figures of first and second husbands Taranis and Esus. On the second panel, god of the animals Cernunnos sits cross legged in the 'Buddha pose', sporting stag antlers on His head, while holding a neck torque, symbol of authority, in one hand and grasping a ram headed serpent in the other. This suggests a figure in control of the chthonic, serpentine forces.

"*A similar [image of a] deity was discovered in the ruins of Mohenjodaro in the Indus Valley, dating back to the third millennia BCE,*" Claire French reports.[14] (Hindu god Shiva is considered lord of the animals, Cows and Snakes in particular, and may well be a continuum of this being.) The origins of

Irish Goddesses and Gods

Above - Cernunnos on the Gundestrap Cauldron.

Indian heritage: Above - Shiva lingams & yonis (male/female symbols).
Below - Laksmi's Holy Cow Kama-dhenhu.

Fairy Haunts of Ireland

Cernunnos must stretch back to the early Palaeolithic people, the hunters and gatherers. In Europe He is seen in various depictions of horned deity figures, often shown holding a purse from which coins are poured, as well as wearing or holding torcs, and accompanied by bulls, stags and a pair of serpents that represent earthy life-force and regeneration. Some rare female versions from Gaul exist too, including a carving in the British Museum.[17] Underworld god Donn is the Irish counterpart to Cernunnos.

On the fourth Gundestrup panel the goddess is apparently depicted as the Queen of Heaven and it's interesting to see her flanked by two Elephants.[14] Likewise, Indian goddess Lakshmi is often shown flanked by two Elephants, symbolising power and water, their colour being white. (She's also associated with Cows, Horses and Tigers.) Lakshmi has three fathers, one being Varuna, a god of the sea and water sources, and symbolic of generosity. Another father, Puloman, is the ruler of the Underworld and the wealth of the Earth. Lakshmi carries a pot symbolising the wealth extracted from nature by human industry; and She is partnered by Vedic warrior god Indra, a king of the sky, wielder of thunderbolts and bringer of rain, who rides a winged Elephant. As well as a golden cornucopia, Lakshmi's other treasures are a wish-fulfilling fruit tree Kalpataru, a wish-fulfilling Cow Kama-dhenhu (seen overleaf) and Chinta-mani, a wish-fulfilling gem. Abundance is assured with these, but Her wealth can bring strife from envy and insecurity, and she is a fickle partner for Indra, always seeking a god of greater wealth or wisdom, such as Vishnu. Lakshmi has two forms. As Bhu-devi she is the Earth goddess of tangible wealth, often shown as a Cow. As Sri-devi, She rules intangible or cultural wealth. Vishnu, in the form of Prithu, became the caretaker of the Earth Cow and ordered that the kings of the Earth should also be Her guardians, as they 'milk' the Earth for Her resources.[18]

According to Irish pseudo-history, after the Tuatha Dé Danaan were defeated in battle they went on to become spirits inhabiting the ancient cairns, a reflection of the practise of depositing bones of ancestors within passage tombs. But back to Danu - She was accommodated into the Irish pantheon by being married off to native Good God, the Dagda. In Europe, Her name (that may have also been masculinised as Don) is found in rivers such as the Danube. But Her memory faded in Ireland. Or did it? Sun goddesses Áine and Gráinne (pronounced On-ya and Gron-ya) are probably later manifestations of archaic Danu. They're best known in the sunny southern regions of Ireland. Áine means delight, bright, brilliant, pleasure, inspiration and melody. Her sister is Gráinne, of the Sun (grian) and the corn (grainne). Áine was considered to be manifest in the landscape, Her breasts - the Paps of Anu, while Lough Gur is Áine's sacred womb.

The Cailleach and the Crane Cult

As a continuum of the crone aspect of the Neolithic triple goddess, the Cailleach has left deep etchings in the bedrock of the Irish psyche. As a creator being, She made significant landscape features from the rocks She carried in her apron/womb. She embodied the greatest of wisdoms, of birth as well as death and rebirth. Birds such as Cranes, Herons, Cormorants and Owls were associated with Her. She lingers in place names and is the wise and powerful old woman of folk tales. But the medieval spin doctors called Her a witch, demon, or the devil's mother. Other such 'demons' are no doubt fractals of this powerful goddess. St Patrick was said to have battled with various female snake/bird demons called the Corra or Caoranach. One senses the legacy of continental female bird/snake beings that were significant to pre-Indo-European cultures; for example - goddesses from the Minoan and Mycenean worlds, to whom rams and bulls were once sacrificed. [19] What's the connection between birds and snakes you might ask? Look at the legs of a bird and you will see the scales inherited from their reptilian ancestors.

Caduceus, the medical symbol of a pair of winged, sometimes bird-headed serpents spiralling up a staff, was the symbol of Sumerian flying serpent creator and healer god Enki, going back several millennia. *"Winged serpent creator gods are a common feature of religion worldwide,"* Michael Tellinger writes.[20]

In his classic 1911 treatise on the fairies, Evans-Wentz mentions that the Egyptian, Roman and Greek gods - *"often declared their will through birds or even took the form of birds; in christian scriptures the Spirit of God or the Holy Ghost descended upon Jesus in the semblance of a Dove; and it is almost a world-wide custom to symbolise the Human soul under the form of a bird or a butterfly."* [21] This seems to be a relic of totemism.

Overleaf - European bird goddess figures include sharp clawed Harpies in Greece and this well known, nearly 4000 year old figure from Mesopotamia, now in the British Museum. The 'Queen of Heaven' Inanna, Sumerian pre-eminent goddess of love, justice, war and fertility, undertook a mythic journey to the Underworld, domain of her older sister Ereshgikal, and returned from it. The end result is an explanation for the seasons of the year, as related deities spend half the year in the Underworld. This clay plaque could well be a depiction of Ereshgikal, queen of the Land of the Dead.

Fairy Haunts of Ireland

Right - The marble sculpture of a bird goddess from Bronze Age Greece sports an elongated, phallic looking neck, that suggests a Crane form.

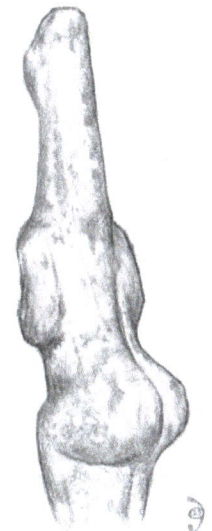

The Crane, that large majestic bird of wetlands, has long been held sacred globally.[19] Similar birds, Storks have also anciently been held sacred to motherhood and, in 'fairytales', are still connected to the birth of babies. Such children's stories often contain archaic mythic elements. Corr, the sound that Cranes make, is the ancient Irish and perhaps pre-Indo-European name for Crane. The Crow is another totemic bird, with great intelligence and its corvid name probably relating it to the death cult also. In Ireland the word for Hooded Crow - badhbh, has an ancient meaning as a female fairy being who takes on a bird form and associates with

25

Irish Goddesses and Gods

certain families.[2] This is a toning down from Badh's former status, as medieval tales of Bodh/Badh (pronounced bov or bav), Morrígan, Neman and Macha as war goddesses described them as "*horrid spectres, often in bird form*" [22].

Corra's name linguistically links St Patrick's enemy demon birds to the Crane. European Cranes in Ireland were slaughtered to extinction by about 1600. Before the Anglo-Norman invasion of the twelfth century it was sacrosanct to kill them, afterwards it was open-season and the iconic bird was easily hunted. (Only now, in the last few years, have they started to come to Ireland again to breed.) In India, a Sarus Crane is sometimes depicted as the companion of the god Vishnu, His lover Lakshmi in disguise perhaps.

Well known patron saint Colmcille (a.k.a. Columba), born 522 AD, was from the ancient Cortraige clan, the 'Crane race', that had the Crane as their totem animal. Colmcille, who was referred to as the Crane cleric, kept a pair of pet Cranes in his church during services, at Glencolmcille in Co. Donegal. This was a place to where St Patrick was said to have banished the flying demons from Croagh Patrick. Certainly Colmcille was involved with some hereditary Crane tradition and was perhaps originally a Druid. Pet Cranes were quite common in those days and they were mentioned in the ancient law text Bretha Comaithchesa.[23]

At Donegal's Lough Derg, originally called Lough na Corragh, Patrick chased the Corra that allegedly swallowed him, but he escaped and killed it. The Corra's bones, as a group of rocks, can still be seen today in the lake. The lough went on to become the most important pilgrimage centre in Ireland. Why was this particular Lough chosen, one wonders? Evans-Wentz reports that, according to the old folks in the neighbourhood, St Patrick was believed to have chased all of Ireland's serpents there. Writing a century ago, he was also told that "*Lough Derg was the last stronghold of the Druids in Ireland.*" [5] Serpents being code for Druids and pagan paradigms, serpentine forms of Earth energy, and the like.

In such purported acts as the 'banishing of the snakes' Patrick's church wanted to say that he'd overcome the indigenous deities, especially those snakey old crone goddesses. But at Lough Derg local folk belief is that Corra still lives beneath the waters, sometimes surfacing during storms and riding its waves like a majestic wild Horse with flowing mane amidst the churning froth. [16] This shows that you just can't keep a good goddess down!

Fairy Haunts of Ireland

Much evidence points to the concept that Corr the Crane was central to the death cult, with the belief that it transported souls of the dead to the Otherworld. Cranes and funerals are linked across various cultures globally. Maiden Roman goddess Persephone had a name change to Kore after she married Hades and became queen of the dead. Perhaps there was a Crane element to Her story too. There's a Crane carving on the base of one of Ireland's finest High Crosses, at Ahenny in Tipperary, dated to the 8 - 9th century, that shows a Crane leading a funeral procession. In China, inside the first Emperor's tomb, thirteen bronze Cranes dating from 220 BC were found; while Taoist priests were once thought to turn into Cranes when they died. Funeral finds of Crane artefacts globally suggest that these birds were widely believed to accompany the dead to the afterlife. In Scotland the Gaelic word Corranach means the funeral cry of the Gaels, which must relate Corra to the wailing Banshee.[23]

Tribal kings were sometimes taken into the heart of bogs for sacrificial killing and disposal, because things weren't going well for the tribe. The nature of the wet, acidic bog environment meant that their remains are amazingly well preserved and some bodies are displayed in museums. Old Croghan Man is Ireland's best example.[24] Although this explanation for his killing cannot be proven, it's considered highly plausible by prominent archeologist Eamon P Kelly.[25] He was a tall, well fed and well manicured individual. Perhaps his soul was sent off along a bog 'corr-idor' to be ushered into the Otherworld by resident Cranes. Associated place names seem to give us this clue.

Wooden bog trackways - toghers, or tochar in Irish - were built across bogs over several millennia, sometimes with great effort and often ending in seemingly random parts of the bog. While many were about linking up access routes with drylands paths, some were probably used as ritual pathways from which sacrifices, of treasures, war booty, animals and people, were made. (In Germany bog pathways have also been found like this, leading out onto bogs and stopping there.) The most famous togher, now well preserved with an interpretative centre built over it, is at Corlea, Co. Longford, and dated to 148BC. The place word corr, usually seen as a prefix, can mean a small hill. But Corlea is in flat bog country. Likewise, a Bronze Age trackway from 1450BC, found by peat diggers one metre below the surface not far from my home in Co. Leitrim, also has no hill there, despite going for a kilometre through the boggy townlands of Corlisheen and Corlona. But a Crane interpretation of the corr in place names remains controversial and unresolved.

An elderly man born in my home recalled how, as a child he helped to dismantle this well made, one metre wide Oak wood togher, as it was in the way of the peat harvesters. There's no trace left now of the trackway that may have lead across bogland to higher ground and on to the fertile townland of Kiltoghert, where the early church of the mysterious St Toghert was located. Kiltoghert could well mean the church of the trackway, rather than an obscure saint, Ordnance Survey researcher John O'Donovan suggested almost 200 years ago.[26] The church, sited near the magic fairy hill of Sheemore, a Bronze Age ritual centre, became the parish church, its importance suggesting a previous Druid stronghold. Was it another centre for the Crane cult?

It's no coincidence that magical Crane connections featured in Druid rituals. For example - *"the bard dons the feathered cloak of the Celtic seer and his prophecies have great authority for the people."* [14] When cursing people with their satirical poetry and spells they stood in a ritual posture inspired by the Crane - standing on one leg, with one eye closed and pointing towards the victim. This was called Corrguinecht, meaning Crane wounding, because it emulated the pose of a hunting Crane. Another legacy of the Crane cult is the mystery tradition of keeping special magical treasures in the skin of one, in a corrbolg / Crane Bag.

Gods of light and darkness

Ireland's earliest known god was the Dagda, meaning Good God, a prototypical Celtic tribal deity. The Dagda has at least twenty six names, according to Eamon P. Kelly and Donn is no doubt a later form of Him. Concerned with the wellbeing of his people, the Dagda had a huge club and cauldron that provided inexhaustible nourishment in the form of cooked meat and oatmeal porridge. He was later deemed to be the father of Lugh, the continental Celtic god of light, who was accomplished in the arts and magic. Lugh, a late Iron Age import, was paramount to the Gauls and lent his name to places such as Lyon (Lug-dunum, Lugh's fortress). Jesus went on to carry the mantle of a being of light; while Lugh's memory faded in Irish folk tradition, whereas the character of His adversary, Underworld god Crom Dubh, lingers on, as does the memory of Donn. The Sun god's last manifestation was in the hero of many legends Fionn mac Cumhaill (pronounced Finn ma Cool), his name Finn giving him the attributes of light, bright and fair-hued.

There was also a trio of lesser known gods in Ireland - Mac Cecht, Mac Cuill and Mac Gréine, described in the Dinshenchas as brothers and grandsons of the

Daghda.[22] On the Hill of Uisneach in Westmeath, Lough Lugh is named for the god Lugh and it's said to be the place where He was killed by Mac Cuill, Mac Cécht, and Mac Gréine.[27] The old gods battling to reclaim supremacy from the new upstart god perhaps?

Examples of possible god figures carved from wood occasionally turn up in Irish bogs. Twenty three anthropomorphic figures, dating from the Early Bronze to Late Iron Age, have been found in eleven wetland sites across Ireland. The Ralaghan Figure has a genital opening, containing a possible piece of white quartz, that's suggestive of an attachment point for a phallus peg, similar to others found in Britain.[28] This is reminiscent of Hindu snake god Shiva, whose symbol is a stone phallus, called the lingam, as seen on page 22.

Crom Dubh

Crom Dubh, whose name means Dark, Stooped One, is the pre-eminent agricultural god found across much of Ireland in historical times. Crom lived in the dark Underworld throughout winter. In summer he ruled the corn fields together with Áine, then left around the 1st August to claim the 'first fruits', in the form of Eithne the corn maiden, bringing her on His back (hence his stoop) down to the Underworld to symbolically germinate the seeds over winter. This ritual 'sacrifice' ensured continuing bounty from the Earth.[16] His traditions vary from place to place and are remembered in fragmented forms.

Called in 19th century sources the god of harvest, Crom's popularity lasted long on the western seaboard, from Donegal Bay down to the Dingle Peninsula and inland, but not between Dingle Bay and Cork Harbour, nor is he mentioned in the north of Donegal, despite these regions retaining much indigenous culture. (But we do often find Donn where Crom is absent.) Crom was sometimes depicted as the last sheaf of corn cut at the end of harvest. An Ulster tradition was the taking of the last sheaf of corn and hanging it up in the home to represent the god (or goddess Cailleach). It would hang over the harvest feast table and was assigned oracular powers. Crom was usually paired up with Áine as the most popular pair of agricultural deities. Eithne, their child, whose name means kernel or grain, had her name anglicised in Ulster as Annie. She is depicted in maiden corn dollies woven from Barley and Oats; their diverse shapes evoking the glyphs of the ancient Sun/fertility cult.

Crom's festival day became known as Domhnach Crom Dubh and Black Stoop Sunday. Later on it was more often called Garland or Bilberry Sunday (for the

Irish Goddesses and Gods

flowers and berries picked), in an attempt to erase His memory. The event was celebrated either on the last day, or last Sunday of July, or on the first day, or first Sunday of August. Over in Scotland there was a curious Scottish saying: *"Di-Dòmhnaich crum-dubh, plaoisgidh mi an t-ùbh"*, meaning - *"Crooked Black Sunday, I'll shell the egg."* [29] The egg association might well hark back to the seeds that Crom Dubh carries and lovingly places in the Earth each year in autumn, when farmers would traditionally sow the next year's crop.

Also called Crom Cruaich and similar names, Crom came with the earliest Neolithic peoples, heralding advances in agriculture. He is associated with Snakes and bulls and may well have originated in India, where the great god Shiva has these same animal familiars. Mairie MacNeill, after a huge amount of research on the subject, concluded that Crom is *"a version of Donn"*, and that also *"he can be regarded as identical with the pre-Celtic food-providing gods Cormac, the Dagda, Elcmar, Midir and Balor"*. Crom later adapted to new technologies, the coming of the Bronze, then the Iron Ages. He wielded the rannach, the staff of life, and was also associated with death. His memory survives in modern times, but only just!

He lingers in legends under various names, such as Black Cormac, Corm Dubh, Crum Dubh, Coirpre, Deodruisg and others. Cormac can be equated as a king of a golden age, which as MacNeill points out *"does not seem incompatible with Crom Dubh,"* whose generous attributes are preserved in medieval tales where He is a provider of food.[22] Cormac was the word for feast. Hence after death the saints are able to win His soul from the 'demons'. Yet the darkness of an Underworld god seemed like the 'devil' to churchmen. Well, eventually it did. At first, Crom's redeeming features were actually praised by St Patrick! He was, in some stories, turned into Patrick's helper and in others, referred to as a *"generous landlord"*.[22]

Lugh, the god of Sun and light arrived in Ireland around 500 BCE from continental Europe with the Tuatha Dé Danaan, or more probably with several invading tribes. Legends cast Lugh as the master, or perhaps introducer, of arts and as Crom's adversary, attempting to wrest the corn maiden Eithne from his back. Together they personified the battle of light over dark, the two halves of the year. Lughnasa, also the name for the month of August, is associated with Lugh, however his influence throughout the indigenous cruthin tribes was negligible and Lugh is barely remembered in local folklore.

Medieval writers dreamt up a hotchpotch of propaganda about Crom Dubh to boost the ascendancy of Patrick's church. There's barely a crumb of truth in their stories, save that Crom was an important enough figure to condemn. For instance, across Ireland a plethora of holy wells that pre-christian pilgrims venerated were said to have been blessed by Patrick, despite him rarely leaving the Ulster region. Some wells still carry the name of the original pagan deities, such as Crom and Áine. Christian pilgrimages to these 'St Patrick Wells' were never held on Patrick's day, but typically at Lughnasa, around August 1st.

After Patrick confronted the god, one medieval story has it, he noted Crom's good works and took possession of His soul, while putting to flight His demons and making Him his servant! Patrick even declared that *"Crom's charities and good works were more than a balance for his sins."* [22] Other stories tell of the 'banishment' of Crom by St Patrick at Killycluggin, near Ballyconnell in far west County Cavan, but they are impossible to substantiate. The Killycluggin Stone found there was said to represent Crom. It's a rounded pillar stone about 1.5m tall, elaborately decorated with spirals in the La Tene style and with its top side missing, as seen below in the Ballyjamesduff Museum in Co. Cavan. It's more likely an inauguration stone for tribal kings. An adjacent Bronze Age stone circle was said to be a centre of Crom's worship, but again, this is purely speculative. The design of the Killycluggin stone carving dates it from the Iron Age and it's missing portion more likely represents inter-tribal warfare amongst Celtic tribes, rather than any act of domination by Patrick.

Crom's chief animal was the bull and His greatest surviving monument is a sacred enclosure for bulls in County Limerick. This is Ireland's largest henge - the embanked arena of Rannach Crom Dubh, otherwise known as the Lios or Grange Stone Circle. Erected around 2500 BC, it's ringed by 113 closely placed megalithic stones and is located near the western shore of Lough Gur, once a significant grain growing and culturally important landscape ruled by Sun goddess Áine. In His most iconic legend, as described by Michael Dames, Crom carries corn maiden Eithne across this sacred site complex from Áine's birthing chair (a limestone slab beside the lake, known as the Housekeeper's Chair) to the Lios. There is an alignment between these two sites on the August 1st sunrise, as well as the November 1st sunset, on an axis of 59 degrees, when sunlight streams down the entrance path into the great stone circle (nowadays this light is obscured, however). The stone-lined passageway on this alignment points towards a pair of horn-like stones, the tallest in the ring. Beneath this stone pair were found layers of organic debris that's evidence of the annual slaughter and feasting on bulls at festivals.[16]

It was along this path each year in the mythic cycle that Crom Dubh entered carrying the corn child, with His spear of life and the seeds of next year's crop, which He symbolically buried in a sacred furrow, marked out in stone beneath the yellow clay surface of the arena. This was enacted on Crom's harvest feast day that was locally called Black Stoop Sunday. The arena may well have hosted bullfighting, ritual battling between groups of men with Ash wood staves and contests of strength. Beneath a floor layer of yellow clay, symbols of the Neolithic god/goddess pair were discovered by archeologists, but not initially recognised. Carefully placed limestone rocks delineate a buried staff 36.4 metres long (the staff being the Dagda's symbol of office as well). There is also a crescent new Moon of the maiden goddess on the same scale. [16]

Crom was often associated with mountain tops and his memory survived longest in wild mountain areas. In 1939 James Hayward noted many Crom traditions surviving in the rugged country between Lough Allen in Co. Leitrim, and Lough Erne in Co. Fermanagh.[30] Nearby, in Co. Cavan, the original Killycluggin Crom stone was found 2.4 km from a hill called Crom Cruach, while at least four other hills associated with Lughnasa hilltop celebrations are known of there. The original pilgrimage to the summit of Croagh Patrick in Co. Mayo was to the sacred enclosure of Crom Dubh and Áine, and this may well have involved a sun-wise perambulation around the summit, as pilgrims do today. Excavations have uncovered structures going back to Neolithic times at The Reek, its nickname, Irish for rick, which is one of Crom's symbols.

Fairy Haunts of Ireland

On the Dingle Peninsula in Co. Kerry, Crom was said to have resided at Ballyduff (Baile Dubh in Irish). Feasting, games and courtship once followed the annual harvest pilgrimage up to the summit of nearby Mt Brandon, the second highest peak in the country and originally called the Mountain of the Dagda. The festival rites, held on Crom Dubh's Sunday, the last Sunday in July, included a solemn cutting of the first grain, then carrying it up to the summit and burying it there, as an offering to the deity. This was followed with a meal of the start-of-harvest food (new Potatoes, grains or berries), at the festival held down in the village of Cloghane on Brandon Bay, 3.2 km from Ballyduff. The sacrifice of a bull may have also taken place, followed by a feast of its flesh and perhaps ritual dance play with a bull hide, plus the usual love making and faction fighting.[22] Medieval legend has it that local hero St Brendan converted Crom to christianity and that this was the reason for the festival - the usual sort of spin we've come to expect!

In the mid 19th century Co. Louth still celebrated an annual harvest festival called the Sunday of Áine and Crom Dubh. At harvest time this divine duo were in their elder aspect and, as co-rulers of vegetation, were ready to ensure the following year's harvest; while their child Eithne sanctified the new seeds for the renewal of life. It's all harmless stuff and no wonder that the early Celtic church was inclusive of Crom Dubh. But in later chronicles we find less tolerance.

Around the time of the Norman invasion in the 12th century, new religious orders swept away much of the vernacular church with its continuum of pagan elements. But then images of Earth deities flowered anew and important building facades started to be adorned with masked, vegetative faces of the Green Man sprouting over them in organic abandon. Churches and castles began to sport carvings of naked, often fearsome looking Sheela-na-Gigs, who appear to represent protective sovereignty goddesses, with a hint of rebellion against the prudish new order. The Green Men and Sheela-na-Gigs suggest ancient landscape / vegetation / fertility divinities and they provided an Earthy expression for an exuberant re-manifestation of Ireland's archaic agrarian traditions. [31]

Irish Goddesses and Gods

Chapter Three
Finding the Fairies

Fairy haunts are ubiquitous across the island of Ireland. They're often found in prominent landscape features, such as on hilltops, in wild woods and holes in the ground, around springs and the like. People once pilgrimaged to fairy places on particular days in the year. Many went to special places such as holy wells to avail of healing 'miracles' traditionally associated with them. Healing effects attributed to visiting these sites may actually be the result of a blessing from the spirits of place. Such knowledge of our true connections to the fairy world has been kept taboo until fairly recent times.

The great thing is that we can still commune with fairy beings today, because they continue to live in a world parallel to our own physical world. It doesn't have to be on a particular day for you to encounter them, nor is the 'second sight' necessary to perceive them or have a special experience of them. Go to these 'thin places' to soak up the atmosphere. If you show your respect and perhaps give a little offering, a token of thanks, you'll be all the more likely to glimpse the fairy world and better appreciate the spiritual reality of place.

In County Sligo

Nobel prize winning author W. B. Yeats spent his childhood holidays with cousins of his mother's family, the Middletons, at Rosses Point and Drumcliff, where friendly peasant neighbours would intrigue him with the local fairy lore, sparking a life long fascination. His uncle George, a shipping magnate in Sligo town, had a maid who was a seer and they both revelled in her tales of the supernatural. Many of the stories he collected for his books were sourced from the Rosses Point to Drumcliff area. When he tried to discover fairy stories from further afield, people were more reticent to share them and he was made to feel like an untrusted outsider. Readers of his stories might get the impression, as his friend the author Evans-Wenz did, that the Rosses Point/Drumcliff area was especially full of fairies or somehow special. However, the tales represent typical fairy/human interactions in the less spoilt parts of Ireland and they also reflect his genuine and life long association with that area. Yeats' intense interest in the fairy world was not necessarily a healthy obsession. He once asked a medium to make contact with the fairy world directly for him. The answer came back to him scribbled on a piece of paper.

Finding the Fairies

"Be careful and do not seek to know too much about us."[32] This is good advice for everyone.

Sligo's iconic mountain Benbulben (seen below) is the subject of many legends. An informant of Evans-Wentz, whose family had lived beside it for 400 years, told him that the mountain is honeycombed with grottoes and is the chief abode of the Gentry in that area. [21]

Near Mullaghmore, on the coastline beside Classiebawn Castle, is a hilly rock outcrop known as the enchanted Dostann na Briona, the Fairy Rock, also called Doras na Briona, the Portal of Dreams. People once put offerings, typically a swig of whiskey or poiteen, into a small round hole at the top of the rock, in gratitude for blessings and at Halloween. They may well still do this.

A famous incident there happened when a violent storm blew up that risked the lives of the fishermen at sea. Concerned people watching from the shore were amazed to see an ethereal white woman standing in one of the boats. She was only seen by them. That boat survived the tempest, while the others sank. Although they hadn't seen her, the grateful fishermen who arrived safely below the castle knew who to thank. They poured whisky onto the Fairy Rock in gratitude for the saving of their lives.[32]

Even non-believers have had fairy encountes in the region of this rock, including the father of author Joe McGowan. As a young lad he was approaching the Classiebawn Castle one evening at dusk when he heard *"music and the clatter of talk and dancing."* He deduced that a party must be going on there, but when talking to the housekeeper she told him there was no party. *"Pay no attention to that,"* she told him, *"I hear that often"*. The sounds were coming from the Fairy Rock, she explained. As he was leaving he heard a loud whistle and, on looking back, saw *"two wee small fellas down under the Fairy Rock and them comin' towards me."* This scared the wits out of him and he ran home at top speed, his hair standing on end with fright.[32]

Knocknashee, meaning Hill of the Fairies, is a large limestone plateau from whose summit other cairn topped hills can be seen. It's a barren place now, but it originally enjoyed fertility and had a much greater population, as lowland areas were either too heavily wooded or too boggy for habitation. The archeological inventory describes a Neolithic settlement there near two possible passage tombs and hill fort earthworks that enclose 21.5Ha on the top. The eastern side has evidence of 30 circular huts from the Bronze Age, these being enclosed by limestone rock cut ditches. There are two large cairns in the north-east and north-west, between them is a circular stone platform.[34]

To reach Knocknashee, from Lavagh village take the Coolaney Rd north-east and pass two roads off to the right. From beside the next house on the left, here the hill is easily climbed.[34]

In County Leitrim

Leitrim's pre-eminent sacred mountain Sheemore, meaning the Great Hill of the Fairies, is a 178m high eminence that's been inhabited for thousands of years and was a royal centre in the Bronze Age. With fabulous views all round, from its summit in fine weather you can see the Sun setting on the summer solstice over Knocknarea in Sligo, 40 km to the north-west. The winter solstice sunrise over Sheemore can be viewed from the summit of Knocknarea.[35]

Sheemore's stately profile is reminiscent of Glastonbury Tor in the UK and it's covered with ancient monuments, including three passage graves, four cashels, three raths, plus ancient field systems, none of which have been excavated by archeologists. A concrete cross was planted on top of one of the passage graves in 1950, unfortunately. The cross remains a pilgrimage point and people often climb up the hill on New Year's Day. It's a wonderful place to visit, if you avoid the area with internet transmitter masts. Although private farmland, there's a tradition of allowing visitors access and this is being maintained by the new owner. The narrow lane to it is very tight for parking, the local council has flagged agreement to build a small carpark nearby.

Sheemore is located on a fertile strip of land that stretches across to Fenagh, another ancient settlement and probably a Druid centre. Nearby (4km east) is the Little Fairy Hill, Sheebeg, at 145m height, with its huge (38m diameter and 6m high), but much disturbed, cairn of quarried stone at the summit. Both hills were made famous by the delightful tune 'Sheemore Sheebeg', composed by celebrated blind harpist Turlough O'Carolan, who was allegedly inspired by fairy music he heard emanating from one of the mounds. Actually, this is another layer of myth, as the well known tune is an older Scottish air.[35]

Sheemore has several caves on the south east side that were fairy strongholds and a fairy queen was said to live in one.[36] Schoolboys in 1935 reported their discovery of a (now lost) stone axe in one of the caves.[37] The cave entrances are very narrow and have possibly been filled in. I've been told of a very unfortunate dog that went into these caves and was never seen again, though it could be heard for a while barking under the ground by its owners above.

Stories tell of how Sheemore was thrown up by giants, who also made a 'bottomless' lake at its base. Some say it was created by Fionn MacCumhaill. A legendary and very loud battle was fought between the fairy hosts of these hills, both led by a giant; while other accounts say they were led by a fairy queen. The two groups flung stones at each other, a pair of which fell in-between the two hills. These remain as standing stones 1.5m high and said to have a pot of gold beneath them, according to folklore collected in 1938. Sheemore gained supremacy in the fairy battle and the next morning *"the domestic vessels in every house in the Sheebeg area were found besmeared with blood"*.³⁸ I find it amazing that there is actually an element of truth contained in this legend, in that the standing stones are very likely glacial erratics brought in by glaciers. So - they did fall from above!

Further to the north, near the village of Killarga, is a glen overlooked by Ben Scardaun, that's sometimes called Lackagh Mountain. People had harvest gatherings there on the last Sunday in July, called Garland or Ben Sunday. Before ascending the mountain they would mass near a little lake, Lough na Wellian, beside two big round stones some 6m high, known as The Sisters. Musicians would play there and people sang. At around 3pm they'd make the ascent to the playing of music and re-assemble at the top around a mound of stones. Berries and flowers were picked, some bunches taken home to be left at doorways to bring luck, and others made into garlands to be left on the summit. People enjoyed their revelries and a bit of faction fighting until sunset. MacNeill tells us that *"children kept close to their parents for there was a tradition that leprecauns used to be seen on the mountain on that day."* ²²

In County Tipperary

Knockshegowna rises to 213m in the centre of a prosperous plain. This is the premier fairy hill in the region, the seat of fairy queen Una, guardian of the local chiefs of the O'Carroll family. On the second Sunday of July, called Garland Sunday, people climbed the hill to pick berries and have hurling matches. Stories tell of fairy revels seen there at night, of men who tried to watch them, who then disappeared; and of how an attempt to plough a field beside the hill ended in disaster.²²

In Count Wicklow

The Athgreany Piper's Stones is a stone circle south of Hollywood and north of Baltiglass, signposted from the N81 road. Athgreany means Field of the Sun. It's a small circle with fourteen boulders. An outlier stone down the slope gives an alignment with the sunrise at midsummer. There's a local legend that fairies play the bagpipes there at midnight. Another story with a christian spin has it that the circle stones were petrified dancers and a piper, the outlier stone, who dared to dance on a Sunday.³⁴ This didn't stop the fairy reveries, however.

Finding Fairy Passes

There are a great many Fairy Passes, but very few are on the record and oral history would know them better. MacNeill mentions one in the mountainous borderland of Co.s Leitrim/Cavan/Fermanagh. Overlooking a bend in the small river Blackwater, that flows from Slieve An Ierainn in Leitrim to the lake at Ballymagauran, near the top of a hill at Bellaleenan is located a St Patrick's Well where Lunaghsa festivities were once enjoyed.[22]

In 1922 a local informant told of a Fairy Pass that goes past this well, within 300m of it, MacNeill wrote. It begins at the hill fort of Derryragh near Ballymagauran and runs through the valley of Glengevlin (- the last inland Irish speaking centre in the country) and onwards to Co. Donegal. Quite some distance! *"The fairies were often heard going the way,"* he reported.[22]

Other stories of Ballymagauran, where Lunaghsa festivities were once held every August 12th, signify its political importance. The Magauran clan (Anglicised to McGovern or MacGowan) were lords of Tullyhaw and with their Druids were probably at odds with the church. This explains why St Patrick was said to go there to confront Crom Dubh, who he flung into a deep hole (sent back to his Underworld home!) It was probably entirely fictional.

Another Fairy Pass in the wild borderland area was recorded by Paul Deveraux, who visited it in 1995 together with a knowledgeable native, the late George Sheridan, plus folklorist Bob Curran. The site, seen on Ordinance Survey map number 26, lies on the Marlbank Plateau, south of Lough Macnean Lower, off the road that runs east from Blacklion. You go down a narrow lane that's signposted as a scenic route to the plateau. After 1.6km or so you take a cement track off to the right, westwards towards Gortaree. 800m before Gortaree a dirt track at a gate goes off to the left, southwards, and this leads to Legalough, a lake on private land. (Deveraux suggested seeking permission locally, or asking at the Belcoo Heritage Centre first.)[39]

The border between the Republic of Ireland and Northern Ireland passes through the middle of the small, circular lake. This remote area has a great many fairy sites and the lake was always considered a particularly powerful fairy area, George told them. *"Until recently, traditional storytellers, the keepers of the lore like himself, held gatherings down at it because they were always so inspired by the spirit of the place."* Sheridan advised that they would say *"By your leave"* as they approached the lake. He also described the path of a Fairy Pass that came off the plateau, past Gortaree, where a few houses were once inhabited by the likes of Sheridan but are now in ruins, and runs down to the lake, in a fold of the land, perhaps following a stream that enters the lough from the east, and partly following the course of the country border.

Another well known Fairy Pass is close by, on the northern face of the Marlbank Plateau, issuing from the base of the imposing Hanging Rock cliff face. The site lies 3.2km east of Blacklion, past the turnoff to the previous site. This is the beautiful Claddagh Glen and it has a car park and information boards. The Claddagh River emerges as a pool at the cliff face and the Fairy Pass runs along the riverbank, on the opposite side to the public path. Both the pool and a cave above it were considered very sheeogy places. The cave was the fairies' emergence point for their comings and goings, and the Fairy Pass was particularly noted for the spectre of fairy funerals that were sometimes seen going along it. Donn MacGuire, the king of the fairies there, was  said to have ridden his Horse into this cave, part of the subterranean course of the river that flows through the Marble Arch caves nearby. It's Donn's portal into the Underworld.[39]

Seven Years in a Fairyfield

In 2015 I came to live in a de-populated corner of Irish countryside amidst tiny Cow fields and empty stone cottages. Tall trees grew out of the hedges surrounding the fields and nature was happy with the neglect of the land. The farmers, who mostly all have day jobs, weren't using agri-chemicals much, so it was a relatively clean, green environment.

It was also a haven for fairies, who can't tolerate chemical pollution, and I called my one hectare of paradise Fairyfield. I gradually got to know many who resided there. I made contact with them on a regular basis over seven years, mainly during my morning meditation sessions. I developed a 'fairy meditation' process of remote viewing that dropped me into their world, let me observe any changes and interact with them. I learned a lot in the process.

I won't disclose the names that I assign to these spiritual beings, as it would be impolite to do so. Uttering the name of a being can invite its presence and if there is no good reason to do this, they won't be impressed, so I'll paint a brief picture of Irish fairy life and they will remain nameless.

Where to begin? Generally speaking there are two groups that I've observed - the summer and winter beings. I watched over seven years as they made their appearances according to the seasons. They're not slaves to particular dates for this; rather, the weather dictates their comings and goings. Until temperatures allow for the emergence of plants and animals, there is no reason for summer fairies to be around. By around May 1st, when the cold and storms have mostly abated, the summer fairies arrive. Having wintered in the Underworld, they are fresh and ready for action.

It was the queen of each fairy territory that I became friends with. To me they appeared somewhat as a white gowned or golden princess. They generally act like a CEO of the fairy company of local beings, ushering in those lesser beings required for biological processes to unfold and working with energies of place.

One fairy queen usually stations herself at the entrance to a geo-vortex that's an earthing point for a Fairy Path. I've surrounded this Fairy Hole with a small stone circle and the 'little people' love to dance there, preferring that I keep the grass short. She'll convey her annoyance if I let it go a bit wild. Like most nature spirits, she also doesn't like the presence of metal in her territory, as it's an 'interruptor of energy', so I have to give her plenty of warning before bringing the lawnmower inside the stone circle and I'm quick to get it out of there when finished. She's delighted with the outcome, as dancing is a favourite fairy activity and a dedicated dance ground needs to be fairly neat and tidy.

One summer's day, when the grass and wild plants had become long and tangled around the perimeter of the stone circle and covered the stones, I decided it was time to chop them back with some hand tools. I had a helper friend, as well as a new German reaping hook that was super sharp. I was chopping with another tool with my back to my friend who, I didn't realise, was getting dangerously close to the Fairy Circle. He had not sought approval for chopping in there and she probably wouldn't give consent anyway. I should have warned him!

Soon I heard a loud exclamation - "*Ohhhhhh*!!!" The blade of the new hook had snapped off! I sent a photo to the supplier and they were aghast. They'd never seen a breakage like that before and they sent me a replacement. When I asked the friend where he'd been chopping I found out that it was actually caused by fairy wrath, not defective metal, and I had to laugh at the powerful lesson he'd received to help overcome his fairy scepticism.

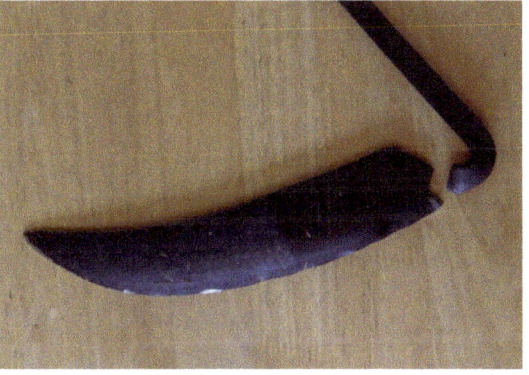

The event was described to me thus. When starting to chop weeds on the edge of the fairy circle, the power in his arm and the previous easy slicing action of the sickle for no obvious reason suddenly became weaker and weaker. A few seconds later the brand new blade just snapped! This fairy queen surely detests the sickle, an ancient tool for taming the wildness of the land and harvesting its bounty. I've never gained permission from her to use it within the fairy circle. While the lawn mower she tolerates briefly, I guess that the sickle harbours traumatic ancestral memories for her species.

Another fairy queen lives across the road, stationed under a vigorous young Oak tree. While the Oak grew rapidly, the original fairy queen had a child (by a sort of cloning) then disappeared, presumed 'dead'. Before she moved on, the

Finding the Fairies

daughter was trained by her mother in the art of dancing and it was such a joy to observe them dancing together. I didn't know then that I'd be losing the queen so soon. But the daughter took over her mother's duties and there was perfect continuity.

A male land spirit rules over a back field that had previously been the home of a stud billy Goat. Usually keeping to himself, no-one was allowed to disturb his little grassy field. He was adamant about that. However if he needed to contact me for a good reason, he'd take on whatever form he felt I'd be open to perceiving, often appearing in the image of characters I'd seen or that resonated with me. Such is the ability of the astral field of these beings, that it allows them to conjure up whatever appearance they want to project, just as we physically choose an outfit from our wardrobe. (And yes, they are influenced by fashion!)

One day, as I stood looking at garden plants, I became aware of the land spirit standing at the side of a path that goes through the food forest. He was in a most beautiful form to behold. To really attract my attention he'd taken the beguiling appearance of Lord Krishna, in a classic pose with a flute to his lips. He beckoned me to follow him. Wondering what it was all about, I followed behind him as he glided up the forest path. Finally he stopped. Right there was a young tree that had been blown over in a recent storm. I was able to lift it and tie it onto something to keep it up. It was a job that no nature spirit could accomplish by itself and a good example of 'co-creative gardening', to use a modern term.

In autumn, when leaves are fallen and things have wound down in gardens, fields and forests, the fairy queens let me know that they're preparing to leave. I start to see a suitcase at their sides, at first just shadowing in. They also start to become fainter to my inner-vision, until one day they disappear.

Then it's time for the land to be ruled by winter beings, traditionally from November 1st - May 1st. In the case of Fairyfield, it's a fractal of the old god Donn, who rides a dark horse and is usually stationed on it beside a vibrant young Monkey Puzzle tree. Donn is the dark lord, protector of place, exuding a majestic benevolent power. He also enjoys riding his Horse up into the sky, often inviting me along for a joy ride, which I occasionally do. It is invigorating to journey with him in the Other-dimensional sky world!

Across the road from Fairyfield, the fairy queen of the warm half of the year is replaced by a fractal of the Cailleach, the crone goddess in winter. When I first perceived Cally (one of Her generic names) She looked something like a stern faced Sheela-na-gig figure (an example is seen on the right).

At first relating with cool indifference, She eventually warmed to me and we made friends. I would honour Her each morning and She might bless me with an energy charge. I often saw Her spinning wool with a wheel, or playing a harp. Sometimes when I listened to Her harping it sent shivers of delight down my spine.

She loved the storms of winter and Hers was the regenerative power of the wintering landscape. She might be a shadow of her former esteemed Neolithic self as the greatest of all deities, but She still exudes great power and authority. I hold Her in the highest respect.

I would be sad to see the last of Cally in late spring, but then I had the delight of dancing fairies to behold. There's never a dull moment in my backyard fairyland!

Finding the Fairies

Chapter Four
Finding the Water Spirits

Water is a dominant force in Ireland, where a large proportion of the land is covered in lakes, bogs and wetlands, and rain is a most reliable resource. Not surprising then is a preponderance of water spirits here. Some water fairies inhabit underwater homes, occasionally contacting Humans on waterbodies, or on the water margins. Others are equally at home under the water as on dry land, according to the accounts of seers and sea tales. Sea fairies, the 'little folk of the sea' abound in the ocean and along the seashore, in rocks and along cliffs. They're traditionally not as friendly to people as land fairies might be.

Beautiful female mermaid spirits pop up all over Ireland. Some are tiny, others are more highly evolved than the average water spirit and may well be manifestations of local sovereignty goddesses. The Folklore Commission has hundreds of mermaid stories in its collection at www.duchas.ie. The stories typically involve men falling in love with Human sized mermaids, but if or when their love and generosity is abused, they return to the waters from whence they came.

Then there are the mysterious Water-Horses, or Horse-Eels that lurk in many an Irish waterbody and are prolific in the watery Connemara region of Galway, as author F. W. Holiday discovered.[40] Described as Horse shaped with a mane and Eel-like tail, some may be remnant populations of Plesiosaurus or similar animals. But, despite many sightings, none have been caught and they may actually be Other-dimensional beings. Lingering spirits of long extinct megafauna perhaps. They remain as enigmatic as their more famous cousin the Loch Ness Monster in Scotland.

Medieval writers referred to them as Worms, in Irish - Peiste or Piast, or Payshtha More, the Great Pest. If this sounds a bit like the proverbial serpent, yes - we might consider them of that ilk. Across the island of Ireland there are countless holy wells, lakes and rivers associated with serpent spirits. (I've written about such primordial water beings in the book Water Spirits of the World.[41]) A good example is my favourite spring well, St Barry's in Co. Roscommon. Energetic analysis of the site finds the serpent force still powering away there, despite a saint's endeavours to banish it.

Mannanán mac Lir

As for the highly evolved water beings, sea god Mannanán mac Lir is Ireland's lord and, literally, son of the sea. Lir or Ler is Old Irish for the sea, while He is the son of sea god Lir. Mannanán rules the waves in the seas around Ireland and the Isle of Man, that bears His name. The three legs of the Manx heraldic arms represent the *"whirling legs of the storm god careering over land and sea."*)[42] Mannanán was considered the father of goddesses Áine and Cleena, as well as many other water spirits. He traverses the waves in a 'self-navigating boat' called Sguaba Tuinne/Wave-sweeper, as well as on Horse spirit Aonbharr / Enbarr, who gallops over the waters as well as the land. Like all good magical heroes, He owns a Crane Bag where he keeps His treasures. Manannán was associated with Aoife, a woman who'd been transformed into a Crane because of jealousy. When Aoife died, He turned her Crane skin into the magic bag, whose treasures were only visible during full tide, and seemed empty when the tide had ebbed.

In Co. Galway, Lough Corrib is one of His legendary homes, while Loughrea is the home of father Lir; Mannin Bay was also named for Him. Place names indicating more of His strongholds include Mannin Lake and Derrymannin in Co. Mayo; Mannin Island in Co. Cork; Cashelmanannan and Sí Mhanannáin / Manannán's fairy mound of Sheevannan townland in Co. Roscommon; and Carrickmannan, 'Manann's Rock', in Co. Down.[43]

Holy rivers

Rivers have their ruling goddesses and many are named for them. Most Irish river names are feminine and many are pre-Celtic and archaic. It was a general rule that names of deities were too sacred to use publicly and only alluded to. Thus in Britain there are six River Dees, named from the word deva, i.e. holy spirit.[44] It's probable that every river has a presiding deity imbued in its waters, as long as the environment is not too polluted. A river is a good place to contact the presiding spirits of water, as water holds their memory and presence, and because spirits are mobile and can potentially manifest anywhere along its course. For example, I regularly encountered a river goddess when walking alongside the River Sihl near Zurich in Switzerland, where I'd been writing this book. I felt her presence touching me from the whole river, like a homeopathic quality infused into it. However, She was usually stationed at an up-river location, away from riverbank phone masts and industries. But She promised to come downstream one day to visit me. And She did.

Meeting a River Goddess

Pushing the stroller slowly as my baby grandson starts to slumber, I stop to sit beside the shallow gushing Sihl River. It's a hot autumn day, the sunshine streaming down deliciously. I rock the stroller rhythmically to and fro. The Sun sparkles mesmerically on the water as I gaze upon it while baby drifts off to sleep, lulled by soothing sounds of flowing water and tree leaves rustling. I could easily drift off myself. Sitting still with baby keeps me rooted in the present and in a meditative state, perfect for reflection and receptivity.

I reflect on the past too, because upstream from here in 1493, in a village called Egg and beside this very same river, the great physician, lay theologian, pioneer chemist and philosopher Paracelsus was born. His classic treatise on nature spirits. 'A Book on Nymphs, Sylphs, Pygmies, and Salamanders, and on the Other Spirits', published posthumously in 1566, was probably the first to focus on this subject. His descriptions of elemental beings were based on ancient and traditional sources. A true Renaissance man, refreshingly -
   "he dismissed the conventional christian view that they are 'devils', instead arguing that nature spirits are significant parts of God's creation, and could be studied just as the rest of the natural world". [45]

Rocking the stroller this way and that is relaxing and hypnotic for me as well as baby. Staring at the sparkling river I sense the energy of the river goddess

Finding the Water Spirits

radiating out from Her golden waters. I'm dowsing the energy with my eyes, inviting it into my being that way. It's invigorating and I revel in the lovely feeling. My mantra becomes:

With my eyes, I drink in the divine essence of the river goddess."

Her seat may be upstream, but the river goddess communicates from a distance. She becomes aware of my presence and tells me that now She will come and pay me a visit. *"How will I know when You are here?"* I ask her. *"You'll know"*, She says. Then I forget all about it and drift back into my reverie. A short while later my meditation is interrupted by a buzz in the left ear - a signal! Yes, She has arrived. I use my eyes to sense the presence of Her auric field. It's now close by. Her energetic being expands towards me, envelops me and is delightful to merge with. We exchange sunny greetings. Projecting love to Her, I receive an energetic blessing back. A few minutes of contact, of being held lovingly within Her field, is a reverie. It's enough for Her. Time to return to the wilder parts that She prefers. I feel honoured and give my thanks.

Some days afterwards I return to the holy river for some fresh air. In the back of my mind I'm wanting a couple of rocks suitable for cracking Walnut shells, as ripe nuts are dropping from the trees. But I wouldn't just take them from the river bank. Rocks provide homes for tiny animals, spirits too; they should be left where they are, unless we have a good reason to take them and get permission to do so. I follow the path of the river, without a conscious thought of rock collecting.

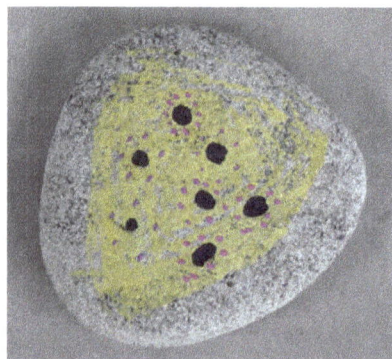

However, sometimes rocks will find us! I look down on the side of the path and see a small flat painted stone - it's perfect for the job. Someone else, maybe a child, has removed it from the riverbank and painted a mandala pattern on it. Yes, it's ok for me to take it, so I do. Later I hold the stone and tune into it. It has a warm, loving energy. I also feel the child's energy within the rock's auric field, the innocence and purity of being. I find myself sinking into a more sensitive state of mind. Then I feel the energy of the river goddess that's also held in the rock. And She speaks to me through it. Ok! Now I have a solid connection to Her.

Fairy Haunts of Ireland

Another day I note the many lovely water washed pebbles on the river bed that could make good pendulum stones. I hope to get permission to take some back to Ireland. I ask the river goddess a few times about it. Each time, I hear "*verboten*". It's forbidden and I must respect Her wishes. She does allow me to take a few on loan, however. They'll all be taken back when I leave, even the painted rock will be returned to the riverbank.

Autumn suddenly turns cold, swathes of tree leaves are falling. One afternoon I feel an urge to visit the river and bathe in the last of the Sun light before it disappears behind the hill. I find the spot where I'd recently seen a man meditating and then dancing on a rock. No-one else is there and so I get to enjoy this riverbank 'sweet spot' undisturbed. Here, right on the river's edge, I sit on a boulder that small mermaid spirits frequent. While Sun bathing, I also Earth myself through the palms of my hands placed on the rock. I'm soon 'in the zone'.

Looking into the clear, flowing waters I watch the low angled Sun rays dance in the shallows, making golden ripple lines flicker across the riverbed mesmerically - a lovely natural light show. Soaking up the divine river essence - a combination of goddess energy, flowing water, bright Sun, warm rock and negative ion rich air - for a half hour of blissful 'doing nothing', I'm reinvigorated and creatively re-inspired. For this, the Irish have a suitable saying, that I've paraphrased in one of my songs: [46]
'tis on the brink of water, that poetry is found.

Right - A male/female pair of Swiss mermaids on a post have long, serpentine tails.

Finding the Water Spirits

In Northern Ireland

Here, the mighty River Bann is named for the Divine Feminine. In Old Irish An Bhanna means the goddess. In his 2nd century book on Geography, Ptolemy recorded the name of the Bann river mouth as Argita, Greek for shining - a most suitable appellation for a river goddess. The river begins east of Banbridge, in Co. Down, flows through Lough Neagh and after forming the border between Co.s Antrim and Derry, exits on the north coast at Coleraine into the sea. Beneath Co. Antrim's fertile basalt soils and within layers of chalk, flint nodules have been unearthed and at Mountsandel on the east side of the Bann River archeologists have found worked flint from Mesolithic times. This is one of the earliest documented habitation sites on the island of Ireland, with hut sites dated to 7000 BC.[34] The river forms a virtual east-west dividing line across Northern Ireland, with the cruithin population a majority to the west of it and the protestant population focussed to the east.

In Counties Carlow & Wexford

Goddess Carman rules the River Garman, that was later renamed Slaney, after Leinster's first king. Slainge was sometimes referred to as Ri (King) Carmain[34]. Others say that namesake Garman was a man, but this seems to be a lazy reading of fable, for the legend cited has it that Garman, whoever he was, spoke of a pregnant woman who enspirits the river. He drowned in the mudflats, perhaps a sacrifice to appease the river goddess?

The river flows for 118 km before entering Wexford Harbour, a.k.a. Loch Garman. One of the Slaney River's two major tributaries, the Bann from Wexford, joins it north of Enniscorthy, where it becomes tidal. The Bann's name is no doubt another from the Irish An Bhanna - meaning river goddess.

In County Kildare

Water god Neachtain, of the Fairy Mound of Neachtain in Carberry, was guardian of the traditional source of the River Boyne at Trinity Well. Medieval pseudo-legend had him married to Boinn, but not happily so. In disobeying Her husband and tasting the well's water that was forbidden to Her, this made the waters rise up in anger and 'drown' Boinn. They flowed out and became the river Boyne. However it's hard to keep a good goddess down and a water spirit cannot drown, only merge into Her territorial waters.

In County Roscommon

The Boyle River, usually translated as Beautiful River, in Irish An Bhuill, has a possible sacred Cow connection. Manchan Magan thinks this name may have been derived from buaib or buaball, which in Old Irish means Cow or ox.[33] The river flows through beautiful Lough Key, where we find three islands that the hag goddess hopped over in legend. Later monasteries and castles were built on them. There are various stories about how Lough Key got its name. One source in 1878 suggested a water goddess, for "*according to the bardic legend, the lake derived its name from a woman named Cé who was the daughter of Manannán Mac Lir.*" [47]

St Barry's Well is located in a pleasant spot in Kilbarry, in the Parish of Tarmonbarry. With its circular stone enclosure and sacred Ash tree, the atmosphere is lovely and peaceful. Barry's original church is in ruins nearby, but the well is in good condition and beautifully maintained. It provides a constant supply of pure water and never drys up.

The place has changed over the years and a description given to the Folklore Commission is quite different to today.

"*On the fifteenth of August every year large crowds of people assemble at this well and pray. There is a very large pile of small stones which were carried there by people who came to perform the Stations. Sick people especially visit this well, as they have great faith in the cure of its water*". [48] This date for the saint's 'pattern day' would indicate a legacy of Lunaghsa festivities. No stone pile remains there now.

The well's legend features a serpent that was allegedly banished by the 5th century saint. Despite this and Barry's concrete effigy standing by on guard for around a century, serpent forces endure there still. The well legend goes that

Finding the Water Spirits

Barry battled a serpent, the Oll Phiast, and chased it to the nearby lough, where it dived in and disappeared.

Another version has it that St. Barry cast his staff before he fell upon his knees and *"felled the monster to earth"*, the water springing up at that spot.

Whatever the case, when I dowsed the site I detected a serpentine energy form rising out of the ground vertically at the well and also an Earth energy current (that some would call a Fairy Line) flowing out from it horizontally, going down the lane that continues on towards the River Shannon, crossing over turf fields and on to the said river lake. It's easily found by dowsing.

Right - a photo snapped by a friend at St Barry's Well has a curious orb with a white cross in it.

In County Cavan

The River Shannon is the greatest river in all of Ireland and the British Isles, spanning a course of 360km. It traditionally originates at the Shannon Pot, a circular pool whose waters bubble up from an underground course beneath limestone hill country in the borderland between Co.s Cavan and Fermanagh. The iconic site, 9km south of Blacklion, off the R206 road, has a magical atmosphere and much mythos attached to it.

One of the river's creation myths is the stock bad-girl story of patriarchal medieval pseudo-legend. It tells of Sionnan, a grandaughter of Manannán mac Lir, who came to the pool to eat the fruit of a forbidden Druidic tree of knowledge, possibly a Hazelnut. This made the waters rise up angrily and She was 'drowned'; the waters flowing out to become Her river.[34] It's another tale to signify the goddess era being suppressed.

Above - Sculture of 'Danu' in Drumshanbo, Leitrim, a river town on the Shannon. (Why not Sionainn, you might ask?)

Manchan Magan suggests the name Shannon could stem from Sean Áine, meaning Old Áine, which is plausible, because it's a stately, slow flowing river for the most part. Certainly the connection with a powerful female is there. Indeed, a century ago T. F. O'Rahilly suggested the river's name could have been derived from Sena, the Ancient Goddess, while a contemporary scholar of his time thought perhaps it was from Senuna, the Old Honoured One. In the 8th century Book of Armagh, St Patrick crossed the River Shannon that the

Finding the Water Spirits

text calls Bandea, meaning goddess.[33] The name Shannon may well have derived from the same root as that of the River Sienne in France.[49]

An archaic creation story of this river was told to Douglas Hyde, Ireland's first president, who was a Gaelic scholar and folklore collector. Originally a great serpent lived in the Shannon Pot and it burrowed southwards from there, creating the river's path as well as its many lakes. It came across other serpents on its way and there were battles between them. The biggest battle left the water red from the blood spilt, which explains the name of Lough Dearg (Red Lake) bordering Co.s Clare and Tipperary.[50] This is an extraordinary record of great antiquity. The same type of story is found across Aboriginal Australia, where landscape features and water courses were said to have been created by mighty Rainbow Serpent Dreaming heroes. Such myths go back tens of millenia! It's also corroborated by many sightings of the so-called Lough Derg Monster,[51] as well as a Lough Ree Monster. These two lakes are the biggest on the River Shannon and a Norwegian researcher who went to Lough Ree in 2001 said the descriptions of the Horse-Eel sighted there are the same as from Norwegian lake sightings.[52]

I can vouch for the presence of serpentine water spirits that continue to reside in the bubbling Shannon Pot today. When I visit, I clairvoyantly see a water spirit family rising up from the depths. With my inner eye I see beautiful mermaid-like beings, with male and female Human torsos and fish tails, which might also be interpreted as snake-like appendages. (Such half Human, half Snake forms may well originate from ancient Vedic culture, as "*anthropomorphic forms of many gods have serpents as their lower bodies*" in the Hindu world.[53] They may have come out of Africa in even earlier times.)

The Shannon Pot mermaids are graceful and noble, friendly and peaceful. They enjoy being recognised by people and briefly interacting with them. No wonder visitors tend to throw coins into the gurgling waters. It's a wonderful, mesmeric place to deeply connect into the spiritual reality of water and nature.

Left - A friend drew a mermaid that she clairvoyantly saw in the waters of the Shannon Pot.

In County Sligo

In Sligo town, below the Sligo Abbey in the Garavogue River, folklorist Thomas Croker noted the tradition 200 years ago of the location of a big black pool called the Linn na Payshta, Pool of the Pest. According to the story, a man dreamed of treasure at the bottom of the pool and dived in on All Hallow's Eve. He found the treasure, but it was guarded by a menacing peiste that looked like a gigantic Eel with a Horse-like maned neck.[54] The same theme recurs in a host of other place stories.

At Lough Gill in County Sligo, lake goddess Gilla was said to be a daughter of Manannán Mac Lir. She sometimes shows herself to people when storms whip up the waters, riding around the lake on Her 'chariots'.[32] A story about Lough Gill collected by the Folklore Commission relates a sense of Her power and the respect paid to Her. It tells of a man who was building a beautiful boat and when it was finished he decided to call it The Lady of the Lake. One day he went out in the boat across the lake and encountered the lake goddess.

"A mermaid appeared to him and she said 'Go back and change the name of that boat. There is only one Lady of the Lake and that is all that there will be'. So the man went home and changed the name. If he had not obeyed the mermaid he probably would have been drowned".[55]

Down the Sligo coastline, the Mermaid Rocks, a few kilometres south of Enniscrone, are a group of round granite boulders in scrub near the road. The legend says that a chief of the O'Dowd clan met a mermaid on the nearby beach, a beautiful fishy maiden combing her hair and singing sweetly. She had a cloak that allowed her to switch between the spirit and Human world. They fell in love, were married and had many children. But one day she went back to the sea, after turning five of the children into the said boulders, while a sixth child became a rock on the shore. Finally she wrapped her cloak around the seventh and together they disappeared into the sea, never to be seen again. The boulders are said to 'weep' upon the death of a member of the O'Dowd clan.[32]

In Co. Galway

Connemara's largest lake is Lough Mask. Mask is the Swedish (Viking) word for worm. There are several water monster stories from here and a dragon-like creature is carved on the headstone of an O'Flaherty tomb in the Oughterard churchyard, marking an encounter with one. The various sightings are typically of a big dark creature in the water that rises up as it swims along, with a couple of humps often all that's seen. Some report seeing a long neck and a bristly mane along it, with a relatively small head that might sport a pair of horns. Similar sightings of unexplained creatures or spirits have occurred across Connemara's many other lakes also.[40]

In County Donegal

On Donegal's north coast, Lough Foyle and the ocean beyond are the domain of Manannán Mac Lir. He rides the waves in stormy weather in His boat the Wave Sweeper. Manannán is said to be 'buried' in the Tonn Banks off the coast of Inishowen, however His spirit naturally persists. I gained a sense of Him myself when meditating on a beach at Inishowen Head. In my mind's eye I saw a strange moving object out to sea, shaped somewhat like a Viking boat. My partner also independently saw this blip on the ocean, but had no idea what it was. I only found out later about the Wave Sweeper boat.

Water serpent memories linger in the Glentogher valley, below the eastern side of Inishowen's highest peak, the 615m Slieve Snaght (Snowy Mountain). The old harvest festival there once involved outings to the summit spring well Tobar na Sul, the Eye Well. Festival goers gathered berries, danced, frolicked and had sports every Heatherberry Sunday in late July. St Patrick was said to have done battle with a tochair, 'serpent demon' in the valley and Plain of the Tochair, and there he established a Church of the Big Serpent Plain, Domnach More Math Tochair.

In County Fermanagh

Lough Erne is named for the goddess Erne. The story goes that young Erne, a priestess of goddess Maeve, was entrusted with Maeve's comb and casket - divine symbols of Her sexuality and mysteries. But she was attacked by monsters and together with Her maidens were all drowned in the lake, Her comb and casket lost.[34] It was a story designed to reduce the import of a local goddess, while concealing some obscured truths. In a more positive interpretation - they were all symbolically incorporated into the sacred lakelands.

Archeologists near Enniskillen excavating a crannog (artificial island home of a high status group) found bone combs buried beneath several hearths. One can be seen in the city museum located in the riverside castle there. The combs were finely decorated and obviously valuable objects in their time. They've been found under other crannog hearths also, an example is illustrated below. The hearth was the sacred centre of the home and such buried combs connected the people with their goddess, anchoring their worldview and sense of homeplace.

In County Monaghan

What must have once been an important complex of sites is found around the ruins of Mannan Castle, on a low but commanding hill spur that's 6km from Carricknacross. Nearby is a holy well, Tobar Lasair, to which pilgrimage was once made and it was famous for curing sore eyes (smokey cottages were bad news for eye health); there's a townland named for a sacred tree, Aghavilla, and also a 'Giant's Grave' megalith there. Mannan, the pagan ruler of the district in legend, whose name is reminiscent of Manannán mac Lir, was allegedly a shape shifting chief who resisted conversion to christianity by St Patrick. Some say he was an 'enchanted man', or a giant.[22] I'd say he was a Druid or water spirit. Legend says that he lived in one of three ponds, marked as Castle Lough on the Ordnance Survey map and the deepest of the three. Mannan's lake had legendary treasure in it and sometimes lights would be seen around it. Attempts to drain the pool failed, due to magical intervention.

Finding the Water Spirits

At the foot of Mannan's hill are the remains of an early christian church, supposedly founded by St Patrick. Typically we find such churches placed deliberately at Druidic sites, to counter pagan practises. St Patrick allegedly struggled against Manann, who, as a shape shifter, attempted to hide from him by taking the forms of a bird, then Hare and fish. Patrick confined his pagan enemy to live in the dark pool. But it wasn't very effective as he's sometimes seen riding around the area on a white Horse.[22]

To get to Mannan's Castle in Donaghmore - from Carrickmacross take the R179 for 4.3km, then follow it around to the left onto the Donaghmore Rd to the castle site, another 1.7km away.

South of the castle lies a natural hollow associated with sacred Cow Glas Ghaibhlean, who could *"fill any vessel brought to her"*. It's called the Hole of Sweet Milk. In local legend, Manann owned the magic Cow and calf and she freely gave milk to anyone in the parish. Some older people became jealous of the Cow's abundance, and an old woman went to milk the Cow into a sieve. This enraged the Cow and she and her calf ran off to Dunany Point in County Louth, where they were turned to stone.[22] Dunany Point, named for Áine, is around 40kms away and was once an important Lughnasa festival site. It was the location for Áine's Fort, now washed into the sea, and one of its stones lying in the shallows is known as The Mad Chair of Dunany. Legends speak of *"the curative nature of the chair and that if a mentally ill person sat on it during a period of lucidity they would remain lucid, conversely if a sane person sat on the chair they risked losing their mind."* The chair-like stone is marked by thick black lines and it can be hard to find amongst all the other stones.[56]

In County Cork

East of Ross Carbery town (2.4km away) is a wedge cairn, visible from the main road, perched up on a ledge below a cliff and surrounded by boggy ground. This dolmen-like monument is known as Callaheenacladdig, the Hag of the Sea. However Ross Carbery Bay is mostly connected with Clíodhna (pronounced Cleena), the paramount water goddess of south Cork. She is said to be the daughter of Manannán mac Lir and is associated with three brightly coloured birds whose sweet songs could heal the sick. 'Cleena's Wave' of legend is the sound of waves rushing into sea caves when the tides come in.

Fairy Haunts of Ireland

Clíodhna's seat is inland, however, for She was a sovereignty goddess of both water and land. Her great rock outcrop, that has an entrance to Her underground palace, is in Carrigcleenmore, 12km south west of Mallow. From this seat She ruled South Munster as queen of the fairies. People reported great gatherings of fairies here, including sighting of Clíodhna herself leading May Eve fairy dancers under the light of the Moon. Cleena's Rock must have once been an impressive site, but quarrying all around it has left it stranded up high in the air with a metal fence around it, a terrible sacrilege, especially since fairies hate metal!

Another special rock with a not-so-well-known Clíodhna association is the Blarney Stone, famous for bestowing the 'gift of the gab' on those who kiss it. It is Clíodhna Herself who bestows eloquence on those who kiss this lump of limestone, now incorporated into the crenellations of Blarney Castle. The goddess is still said to exert influence on particular families in Munster who claim allegiance to her, especially the O'Donovans and O'Collins, who ruled Her territory from the 4th to 10th centuries. When the MacCarthys and Fitzgeralds took over from them, She re-aligned to the new order and became known as the Banshee for those families.[2] Other ruling families around the border with Kerry, the O'Keeffes, MacAuliffes and O'Callaghans, also considered Her the goddess of their tribes.[22]

Serpent Lake, Gap of Dunloe, Killarney, Ireland.

Above - a postcard collected by the author's grandmother in the 1960s..

Finding the Water Spirits

Above - meditating at the peaceful Shannon Pot. An interpretative (tourist) centre is planned to be built close by in the near future.

Chapter Five
Finding the Sun Goddesses

Sun goddesses have been very popular in the soggy land of Eire. The Sun determines crop growth and well being, and venerating it here is entirely understandable. Áine is the most well known Sun goddess of sovereignty and agriculture, and She's particularly beloved across the sunny southern province of Munster. Áine rules the waters as much as the land, for the abundance gleaned from Earth's fertility depends on both. This 'mother of the gods' has Her homes on hilltops and in lakes. She is found under various names and guises across the island of Ireland and though She may have been demoted to a 'fairy queen' in medieval tales, we know Her original status was pre-eminent.

In County Limerick

The Lough Gur area is central Áine country. The lough itself is Her principle birthing lake and the name Gur could mean birth pangs, suggests Dames. Here She was entreated for the successful birthing of the golden crops of corn (grain) and locals once considered Áine their ancestor. They reported many sightings of Áine, who manifested in various forms - as an old woman, royal maiden or mother; or as a mermaid living in a bright underwater city. Often Áine was observed standing half submerged in the lake water combing Her long hair.

On the western shore of the lake's largest island Knockadoon, beside the shoreline path is one of Áine's favourite stations. A flat limestone slab there, known as the Suidheachán / Housekeeper's Chair (or Suidheacán Bean-a'-tighe)[57], is where Áine likes to sit and selectively reveal Herself to people, looking *"every inch a queen,"* one man said. Occasionally they witnessed Aine combing Her golden hair with a golden comb there. In 1971 a man reported that She still sits on the chair thus, and that *"she'll continue to do it for all time"*. The comb is an archaic goddess symbol, Dames points out, mentioning ancient Greek rites of Earth goddess Ge-Themis, that were centred on a comb (kteis) - *"which was regarded as synonymous with the female pudenda, from which she gave birth to the Sun and the Moon."* [16]

Folk tales of Knockadoon tell of a cave that's an entrance to the Otherworld of Tir N'a Og, the Land of the Dead, where an old man and woman lived. While Áine presided over the growing corn crops, death was the other side of the coin and also Her domain. An alternative name for the lough was recorded

Finding the Sun Goddesses

amongst local folklore for the Schools' Collection as *"loc-na-gcorr which means the lake of the herons or cranes"*.[58] This would suggest a place for death rituals and the following story reinforces this.

"On the 6th night of the full moon the people brought their sick close to the lakes so that the moonlight shone brightly on them near the waters of the lake. The old people called this night 'All-Heal' and if a sick person was not better by the 8th or 9th day of the moon he would then hear the 'Ceol Side' [fairy music] which Áine the bean-sidhe [banshee] and spirit of Lough Gur would sing or play to comfort the dying. The sick person would fall asleep...to the whispering song of sleep which Áine's brother Fer Fí played. Fer Fí was a kindly red haired dwarf and it was said to be a sign of good luck to hear him laughing."[59]

Áine's hilltop seat is at nearby Knock Áine, between the villages of Bruff and Hospital. The summit has the ruins of a cairn and three barrow mounds dating from the Neolithic and Bronze ages. These barrows were claimed to be tomb residences of ancestral spirits of the Eoghanachta, tribal rulers of a much later era. It was here that their kings were inaugurated, having gained Áine's blessing.[34] Another case of invaders using cultural appropriation! The older summit cairn was regarded as Áine's home and Underworld entrance, a portal that would open on the eve of Celtic festival days with fairy appearances there common, especially at Her power time of mid-summer.

Annual ceremonies on the night of the summer solstice saw a great gathering of men coming from far and wide. They gathered with flaming torches of hay and straw and marched in procession sun-wise around the hill and mounds, then through the fields of corn, waving them around to bring luck. This ritual was enacted until 1879 and it was said to emulate what the fairies were doing, sometimes led by Áine, their queen. Áine also sometimes manifested as an old woman, who might ask for a modest favour. If treated well, She returned the favour with good fortune.

To visit Knock Áine, turn in towards the hill by Knockainy post office and follow the road as far as the school. There is no special track up to the summit.

Knock Grean / Cnoc Gráinne is another Sun goddess hill, situated north east of Lough Gur between the villages of Pallas Grean New and Pallas Grean, and named for the palace of Sun goddess Gráinne, sister of Áine. Carey Reams describes this hill as having the loveliest atmosphere of the three famous fairy hills of Limerick. The hill was also known as Knockseefin, the hill of Fionn's fairy mound. But it was first and foremost a power place of the Sun goddess.

Fairy Haunts of Ireland

Pallas Grean is just off the N24 Limerick to to Tipperary road. Find a way up through the fields to the top of the hill, there is no particular path. [34]

In County Kerry

Crobh Dearg, meaning Red Claw, was a Goddess in north west Cork, with a station at the eastern edge of the Co. Kerry border with Cork, on a ridge of the Derrynasaggart Mountains. A well at a mountain pass was called Cathair Crobh Dearg / Cahercrovdarrig, named for the red haired goddess and locally called The City. The ancient stone walled enclosure, or cathair, has a 157m circumference, within which is a ruined megalithic tomb, an ogham stone, an earth mound, a holy well that "*noisily bubbles up from its depths*" when the water table is high, a penitential station, a primitive cross-inscribed stone altar, a 19th century cottage, and a modern statue of the Virgin Mary. Here, each May Day/Beltaine, a 'pattern day' was celebrated (the christian version of pagan festivities), centred at The City's holy well, when cattle were once brought in from miles around and driven through the well waters to keep them safe for the following year. Later on they would simply make the Cows circle around the well. The annual May Day festival here continued up until World War 2 and involved people circling the well, music, dancing, drinking, and "*champions...performing feats of valour.*" In 1983 music and dance were reintroduced to the May Day festival at Cahercrovdarrig.[60]

Not far from Killarney and visible from The City in the Derrynasaggart hills are the famous Paps of Anu, Dá Chích Anann, the breasts of Anu - a pair of rounded peaks each around 690m high, that look very like breasts. Long considered sacred to the goddess, the summits each sport cairns that, from a distance, look like "*stone nipples on the great breasts of the mother goddess.*" There's also a line of stones, called Na Fiacla, connecting the two mountain tops that's believed to have been a processional route.[61]

The Paps are a 26km drive from Killarney off the N22 road, exiting at the village of Clonkeen; or they can be accessed from Rathmore via N72 road (10.8km), or you can trek to the eastern Pap in less than 2 hours from The City, the path traversing some difficult terrain, with boggy areas and a zigzag course through thick Gorse scrub.[60]

A trio of holy sisters were also associated with this region - St Latiaran, Inghean Bhuidhe (yellow haired) and Lasair (flame); or in earlier tradition - Anu, Badhbh and Macha i.e. the triple goddess.

In County Cork

Cullen village has more strong traditions of the demoted trio of goddesses, St Latiaran, Lasair, and Inghean Bhuidhe. Alternatively, Latiaran's sisters were said to be Crobh Dearg and Gobnait, the Bee Goddess, later a saint. *"It's interesting that Gobnait is remembered in February, Crobh Dearg in May and Latiaran at the end of July - covering three of the Celtic festivals,"* Meehan notes.[34] Latiaran's Well is in an old graveyard at Cullen and on her pattern day, July 25th, people went there to 'do the rounds', curtsie at a heart shaped stone, drink the well water, dance and frolic. Legend has it that the three sisters eventually disappeared down into the ground, after which three springs/wells then appeared, at Cullen, Cahercrovdarrig and Ballyvourney. Spiritual acts often cause water to manifest, this mystical effect is well established (pardon the pun).

Not far from Mallow, Goddess Clíodhna has Her inland stronghold in a clump of unassuming grey boulders in the townland of Carrigcleenmore. Cleena's Rock/ Carraig Clíodhna is the entrance to Her Underworld palace in the hill from where She was said to have ruled as queen of the fairies of south Munster. *"The place is a mass of rock reaching in some places to a height of fifty feet and covering about two acres,"* the Folklore Commission story goes[62]; but, tragically, quarrying has all but destroyed the site. Cliodhna was described as *"a beautiful lady who is said to have appeared on top [of the rocks] very often on summer evenings long ago, and on these occasions she was always engaged in combing her hair with a silver comb."*[63] There were reports of regular gatherings of all the fairies at this spot, while many people claimed to have seen Clíodhna leading the May Eve dance with her fairy followers by the light of Moon.[2] The Rock, as locals call it, is 12.7km south of Mallow via the N20 road, after 5.6km turn right onto the Old Mallow Rd.

Aeibhill, sister of Clíodhna, lives in an underground palace at Castlecor, near Kanturk, beneath an old cave hidden by trees. She assumes Her form as a beautiful maiden for a week each year at midsummer and was considered the guardian spirit of the Dalcassian tribe, as well as queen of the fairies of north Munster. King Brian Boru was reported as saying on the evening of the Battle of Clontarf that Aeibhill came to him the previous night and told him that he would die that day, which he did.[64] Another source says that Clíodhna had two sisters Bína and Maeve, suggesting the triple goddess in disguise again.

"On one occasion she became so jealous of Bina having captured the affections of a handsome young man in the vicinity, that she condemned her to live forever in the form of a white Cat in the caves of Castlecor".[65]

In County Tipperary

The Rock of Cashel is a striking landscape feature, a rocky outcrop originally held sacred to Mor Muman, another sovereignty goddess of the south. Kings of Munster province had their royal palace there from the 4th century, ruling over the lesser kings. It was the top political power centre of the south for the Eoganachta dynasty and where their over-kings were inaugurated - always seeking the consent of the goddess in the process. In the 12th century a descendent of Brian Boru handed the castle over to the church. Glimpses of its earlier sanctitude remain. In the Hall of the Vicar's Choir, a restored 15th century building, a St Patrick's cross has been firmly planted on top of the extruding rock base. Here, via a mirror, visitors can glimpse below this sacred stone into a deep recess that may well have been a cavity providing a goddess Underworld portal through which the right of kingship in Eoganachta inaugurations was affirmed. Nearby a carved stone Sheila-na-Gig evokes the goddess of fertility and territorial sovereignty.[34]

To the north west, twelve small rocky mountains known as the Silvermines are associated with goddess Ebhlenn/Evelyn. They've been mined for minerals since the Bronze Age and the foothills are dotted with megaliths. In the centre is a small peak called the Mother Mountain, with a cairn of small stones on top called the Terrot. Climbers passing it leave a stone there. It was a Lughnasa festival site until the 1920s.[34]

In the south-east lies the Slieve na mBan/Slievenamon/Hill of the Women, that has associations with Fionn MacCumhaill and fairies, as do the Galtee Mountains in the south-west. One legend of Fionn mac Cumhaill tells of him meeting a dwarf when walking on Slievenamon. The earth elemental being played sweetly on his harp and he never left Fionn's side from then on. He taught musicians his fairy tunes as well and they found him a wife who could see the future. These two dwarves plus Fionn's Deerhounds were counted as the 'Three Blessings of the Fianna'. Fionn took good care of the dwarf pair and when weather was bad he kept them under his mantle. To the author this detail sounds like the action of deities and nature spirits, who often carry lesser beings under their mantle, i.e. tucked into their auric field.

Another Fionn story had him out hunting near Slieve na mBan where, beside a spring, a beautiful woman approached him, filled a silver drinking cup for him and left without a word. He secretly followed her to a door in the hillside, which opened up and she went inside. Fionn lunged in after her, but the door slammed shut before him and his thumb was caught. He managed to get it free and put it in his mouth to soothe the pain. From then on he had the 'second sight' whenever he sucked his thumb.[34] (There are similar versions of this story for other locations.) Fionn must have encountered a Goddess, or a spirit of initiation.

In County Tyrone

Around the fertile Clogher Valley there are many Other-worldly sites. Knockmany Hill boasts the remains of a 5000 year old passage tomb known as Anya's Cove. Only the circle of stones remains, six of its 1-2m high orthostats are highly decorated with lozenges, zigzags and concentric circles, similar to the tombs in Loughcrew and Newgrange. The cairn faces due south and towards Loughcrew, some 80km away. In literary tradition it's the grave of Queen Baine (whose name some translate as whiteness) and in local tradition it's the home of the 'fairy' Áine, as well as female giant Una, wife of giant Fionn Mac Cumhail.[66] It's location is off a hilly road that's locally called Mad Woman's Leap.

Originally covered with a cairn of stone and earth, the tomb was enclosed in a concrete shelter in 1959 by the Department of the Environment to stop more deterioration from the elements. A cairn was put over this to give it a more original appearance. A key needed to gain access inside can be obtained from the Northern Ireland Environment Agency. However, if you don't have a key you can still view the stones, through the entrance and also from above, through the skylight on top of the cairn. To get there from Ballygawley, go south on the A4 to Auger, turn right at the roundabout onto Knockmany Rd. At the Ballymagowan crossroads turn right and go uphill, go right at the fork, then take a sharp right toward the woods. From the car-park you can walk to it along a trail through Knockmany Woods, with wide views of the Clogher Valley below. [67]

Close to nearby Clogher, on a slight rise in the valley floor, an ancient earthwork was once the inauguration place of the local kings. At Slieve Beagh 6.4km away, Altadavin (meaning height of the demons) was the site of an annual Lughnasa assembly held on the Sunday following July 26th, the same date as the Old Clogher Fair. The glen below this has a chair shaped boulder that's associated with demons and serpents. St Patrick allegedly banished these spirits into nearby Lough Beag. Connected to the fair was the annual Clogher Mountain Hunt, an event of archaic significance where men and their Dogs met at the Fair and spent the day in the hills hunting Hares. The Clogher Valley remained a Gaelic stronghold until quite late, up to 1607 and the earlier pagan importance of the area is confirmed by its choice of location for an early abbey, Clogher giving its name to the diocese. A stone from pagan times with reputed oracular powers was installed into a fifteenth century church, the Clogher Cathedral, and can still be seen today on its porch. The name Clogher /Cloch Oir means golden stone, a reference to it having once been encased in silver and gold, although the present stone may not be the original one. Indeed, according to an information panel there '*some authorities consider that it may be the lintel from the door of an 8th or 9th century church*'.

In County Armagh

Emhain Macha, named for sovereignty, fertility and war goddess Macha, was Ulster's pre-eminent royal capital. It sits on top of a low hill 1.8km west of Armagh city. The name was anglicised as 'Owenmagh', which became corrupted to 'Nawan' and eventually 'Navan'. Also called Navan Fort / Rath, the hilltop enclosure is marked by a large bank and ditch encircling the hill, featuring a ditch on the inside that appears to indicate a ceremonial centre, rather than a defensive wall.[68]

Inside the enclosure are the remains of structures including a huge roundhouse that suggests a temple. This was a timber structure that was subsequently filled with stones and burned down, then covered with earth to create the mound that's seen today. The site's importance was greatly embellished in the tales of the 'Ulster Cycle', according to more modest archeological findings, suggesting its use to bolster the supremacy of particular Ulaidh clans.

A famous legend of Macha's alleged downfall links Her with Horses. It was traditional to view the passage of the Sun as being assisted by divine aerial Horses. This goes back to ancient Vedic roots, as Indian Sun god Surya is said to go on His daily rounds from east to west on a chariot driven by Horses.

In the put-down legend, Queen Macha is forced to race against Horses when heavily pregnant and died in childbirth as a result, before which the men of Ulster were cursed by Her to suffer pangs of childbirth and weakness at times of danger, for nine generations.[34] It's signals a violent patriarchal re-ordering of a more matriarchal cruthin world-view.

Finding the Sun Goddesses

In County Westmeath

The Hill of Uisneach is a series of undulating limestone outcrops rising to 183m, thought of as the centre of Ireland and a pivotal point situated 24km west of Mullingar and east of Ballymore. It commands sweeping views over the flatlands and was once the setting for assemblies and huge seasonal bonfires from Neolithic times up until the Iron Age. These have been reinstigated in recent years. Like other assembly places, it was said to be the burial place of a great goddess. Ériu, the sovereignty goddess who gave her name to the island, is said to be 'buried' beneath the Cat Stone, also called the Stone of Divisions, which lies on the south west slope. The concept of a national geography of five provinces is relatively recent to this site. Certainly the island has been beset by strong political divisions and competing narratives. Like so many other sites, this omphalos stone has layers of mythic meaning and overlay, like so many other sites. Earthworks found around the hill were probably ritual enclosures, while remnants of ancient roads converge here, one running south, another to the north.[34] Modern pagans go to the Hill of Uisneach to celebrate seasonal events, with traditional Bealtaine celebrations revived in 2009. The Uisneach Fire Festival continues to take place on the 6th of May every year. A tour of the site, that is privately owned farmland, is the only way it can be accessed.[69]

In County Galway

Several enigmatic stones, beautifully decorated in the Swiss La Tene design style, are a key to Iron Age Celtic royal customs in Ireland, although they are barely known, nor recognised in populist pseudo-mythos. The stones were probably brought to Ireland by tribes from Europe. In Germany's Rhinelands several similar stones were found and also some in Brittany. These beautiful stones must be the true 'Stones of Destiny' mentioned in the medieval literary annals and said to be brought in by the Tuatha Dé Danaan tribe. As stones of inauguration, they would have been related to the symbolic marriage of a new king to the sovereignty goddess. The most famous is the Turoe Stone from Turoe, Co. Galway, a 1.67m tall granite stone that's been removed from public viewing for years now, but is destined to return again to Turoe Farm in Bullaun village, near Loughrea. It is key evidence for Turoe (a.k.a. Tara) being the first royal centre of Connaught and it was found inside the nearby Rath of Feerwah, home of the father of pseudo-historically-infamous Queen Maeve. The Turoe stone is considered the finest example of its kind in all of Europe.[49]

Below left - Ptolemy's 1st-2nd century map of Ireland only showed two royal centres (regia), one for Ulster in the north east and the one in Connaught at Turoe/Tara, near Athenry (ford of the kings), home of the Gangani tribe, where the Turoe Stone (below) was found. (Other tribal and place names have been omitted.)

In County Roscommon

In Roscommon the gorgeous Castlestrange Stone, a 60cm high egg shaped stone, is the other best example of the seven known 'Stones of Destiny' in Ireland. Fortunately for the spiritual pilgrim, it is publicly accessible. It sits forlornly and out of context, having been made an estate ornament at the entrance to the grounds of the now derelict Castlestrange House, near Fuerty, 9.6km south of Roscommon town. It's beautifully decorated and there is more to it than meets the eye.

One day when visiting the Castlestrange Stone I was enchanted to clairvoyantly see a small spirit in mermaid form stationed on top of it, looking to me just as Áine has appeared to countless past percipients at other Sun goddess sites. This stone doesn't just hold the memories of kingship rituals, that involved a symbolic marriage with the sovereignty goddess who rules the waters as well as the land. It also acts as an anchor, a station for Her continuing

Finding the Sun Goddesses

presence in the Other-dimensional world and as a portal for Her to interact with our world. I felt so privileged and grateful for Áine for choosing to reveal Herself to me that day.

In County Longford

The legendary 'fairy mound' of Ardagh Hill/ Brí Leith, the locally highest eminence at 198m height, is the god King Midir's Underworld home. Here Etain, pronounced Aideen, the wife of Midir, also lived. Sometimes seen by locals on the old fair ground there, Etain was described as a queen with flaming golden tresses and a bright comb of silver and gold - a true Sun goddess I'm sure![34] She is sometimes known by the epithet Echraide - Horse Rider, which reinforces a Sun connection too.

Her well known myth, the 8-9th century saga 'The Wooing of Etain', is reminiscent of that of Greek Underworld goddess Persephone, who was taken into the Underworld by King Hades. There is a love tug for Etain between Midir and the cultivator King Eochaid, of Frewin Hill, in the role of Greek king Triptolemus, of the thrice ploughed furrow. Persephone's journeys in and out of the Land of the Dead explained and ensured the cycles of Earthly fertility through the seasons of the year. (No doubt the medieval monk writers knew the classical myths and were not shy to borrow their themes to embellish Irish stories.) At one point in their story, Midir and Etain elope off together in the form of Swans, another archaic reference.

In historical times the hilltop has been a focus for annual Lughnasa festivities on Bilberry Sunday. An old track up the hill has lately been resurfaced, along with the instigation of a Bilberry Sunday Walk. Since 2012 this has been held on the last Sunday in July from around 11am, to remember the tradition of Bilberry Sunday. The path is planned to connect with the Corlea trackway and the canal walkway from Kenagh, and it will be called the Midir and Etain Trail, for the connection between Ardagh and the trackway. In legend, a bog trackway was made as the result of a forfeit Midir had to perform for King Eochaid, after losing a game of Fidchell to him. It's a speculative attempt to explain this prestigious trackway, which would have been the undertaking of a huge number of people, so the tale would certainly not pass a Fact Check.

Ardagh Heritage and Creativity Centre, situated in the old village school house, is worth a visit (you may need to book ahead). It celebrates the legends of this mountain and is a very fairy friendly place.

In County Offaly

Croghan Hill is a low volcanic eminence rising up from a vast bog and featuring ancient mounds. Its Bronze Age fort with four embankments and ditches indicates a high status site that was used over subsequent millennia. In the late Middle Ages it became the inauguration site for kings of the Ui Failghe tribe, who gave their name to Offaly. Here they may have symbolically wooed the goddess Eile whose home it is, the ancient place name being Cruachan Brí Eile[2]. There are tales of 'the men of Ireland' coming to woo the beautiful Eile here, with many of the rejects meeting a grisly end. This could be related to sacred kingship protocols of the past; perhaps a warped fragment of memory of the deposition of kings that didn't usher in fertility and plenty for their tribe. When hard times struck, the king would be replaced. First he might be ritually killed in several different ways, then deposited into the sacred bog, possibly off the end of a togher (wooden bog trackway), where his soul could be collected by majestic Cranes and whisked away; Cranes being agents of the goddess of death.

Bog bodies were virtually pickled or tanned in the highly acidic bog water, with only the bones dissolving. And thus the well preserved body of 'Old Croghan Man' was unearthed from the peat at the base of this hill in 2003,

Finding the Sun Goddesses

having met with his fate sometime between 400 to 200 B.C. His leathery, naked body, 6ft 6" / 1.98m tall with well manicured nails and fingers that show no evidence of manual labour, suggests a member of the social elite.[24] A very unlucky king, no doubt.

The incoming christians seized upon the importance of Croghan Hill and put their own establishment there, an abbey associated with St Brigid. Another medieval story tells of St Patrick at an assembly of bishops encountering two powerful females there. Fair haired Eithne and red haired Feidheilm had come to a well on the hill and he supposedly converted them. Through this typical propaganda, the theme of the powerful feminine hangs on slender threads from the pagan past.

Croghan Hill is a portal to the Underworld at Samhain (October 31st), but people were diverted away from this by the alleged miraculous creation of St Patrick's Well.[2] However, it's likely that a holy well sacred to goddess Eile was already there. You'll have to assess this possibility yourself. Find Croghan Hill south-east of Tyellspass towards Daingean. The well is up a small laneway on the hill, inside a walled enclosure.

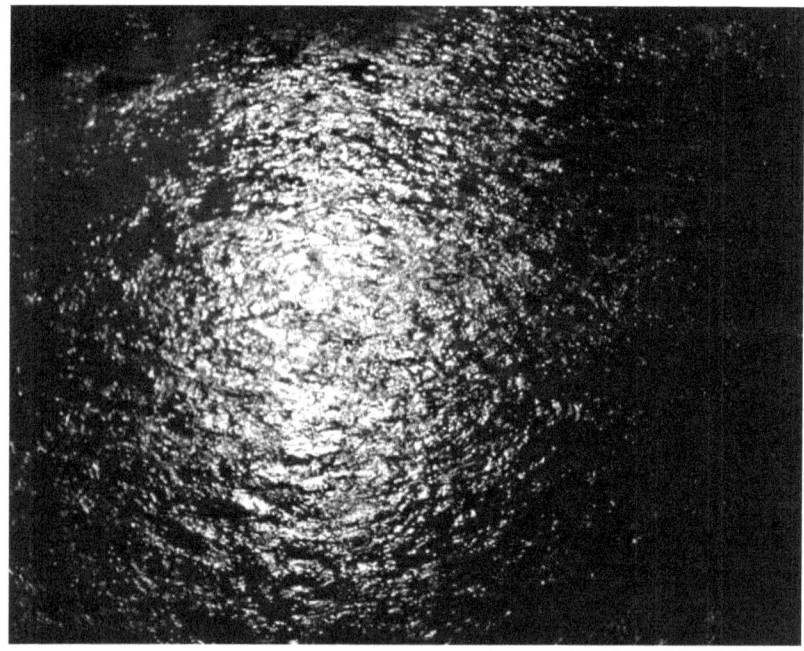

Chapter 6
Finding the Mountain Gods & Heroes of the Divine Masculine

Behind every magnificent Goddess, there's a good god as her partner. Irish deities were grouped in families as well and there was a certain amount of equality between the sexes, mirroring the structure, gender roles and social mores of Celtic society. Many Irish legends feature male heroes who epitomise the Divine Masculine as noble agents for the protection of sovereign territory.

Originally cast as providers of sustenance and wellbeing, these supernatural warrior figures evolved from Neolithic agriculture gods who won over the fertility of the land only through courteous co-operation with its goddesses. Later, kings of Celtic tribes emulated the gods and if disaster struck the crops, it was they who paid a high price for not keeping the ancient bargain, forfeiting their lives and becoming the ritually slaughtered, royal bog bodies that are sometimes dug up from peat swamps.

One of Ireland's oldest native deities, Donn the 'Dark One' is an Underworld spirit long associated with mountain tops, fertility of the crops, the weather, as well as death. He rode or flew on a Horse in the sky and pronounced weather omens. As king of the dead, locals would fear the sight of His white Horses galloping by on a stormy night, as it could mean that their death was imminent. Like horned god Cernunnos, Donn was also a god of animals.

In a medieval tale of Fionn and his Fianna warrior clan, one day while hunting Deer in ancient Oak woods they came across a huge stag who spoke to them. He told them that he was King Donn, the herdsman of all the Deer, and that they should spare his life. But they killed Him anyway.[70] Which was one way of saying that under the searing new light of christianity, a new order of mythos, of Finn - the being of white/light, had extinguished the old, dark Under-worldliness that was Donn.

In County Limerick

At Donn's home on Knock Firinne/Feerina, one of the most famous fairy hills in Munster, he was called Donn Firinne. At 290m, Knock Firinne is the highest

Finding the Mountain Gods

hill of a ridge of old sandstone, with sweeping views over the fertile fields of Limerick. It has a hilltop cairn, a dolmen/wedge cairn on the northern slope known as the Giant's Grave, plus an old rath on a jutting ridge known as the Fort of the Fianns (Fionn mac Cumhaill being remembered here as a giant.) In folklore from a century ago, Donn was regarded as the king of the fairies and as a giant who was 'buried' beneath the big cairn on the summit. A deep hole in the hill, called Poll na Bruidhne, was said to be an entrance to His palatial home, from where strange sounds and music sometimes emanated. Stories tell of underground tunnels from His great hall that led to the Shannon River, Tory Hill and other places of Donn's frequent.

Sometimes mortals that Donn favoured were permitted entry into his Underworld home, one was even allowed to take back a supposed-dead brother and sister to the land of the living. Folklorist MacNeill wrote that here -
"no place in Ireland has maintained a livelier tradition of a fairy king"[22]. Fairy king being politically-corrected-speak for a powerful God of yore, who, though belittled, was at least not forgotten.

Locals would once look to the hill to foretell the weather. In 1825, folklore collector Thomas Crofton Croker was told that -
"people connected the Firinne [meaning truth] element of his name with weather omens: they said that Donn collected the clouds on his hill and held them there for a short while to warn of approaching rain, and from the reliability of this sign came his name, Donn of Truth." [54]

On August 1st, an annual Lunaghsa festival was once held on the hilltop and offerings of fruit and flowers would be left there for Donn and his fairy hordes. In the evening, on a flat area near the summit, young people would dance beside a bonfire and fairies were reportedly seen frequently. They were typically described as looking like little girls dressed in bright blue. One informant called these *"little angels"* and explained that they were only seen on the eves of May Day, Lunaghsa and November, when fairy gifts would be left there for them.

Stories tell of the fairies of Knock Firinne, led by Donn, fighting each autumn with the fairies of Knock Áine, led by goddess Áine. They would have a hurling match and the winners would enjoy the best Potato crop.[16] If people in the area found signs of blight on their Potatoes they would say that Don Firinne and His fairies had been fighting there the previous night.[22]

In County Fermanagh

Benaghlinn is a hill in a range on the western side of Upper Lough Erne. Once the location for hill-top Lunaghsa harvest festivities, people would enjoy sweeping views from the summit of the territory of the Maguire clan - labyrinthine lakelands within a green patchwork of farm lands, and to the south, the dark desolate highland moor country of the Quilca Range. Locally called Bin, it was known to be a special fairy place, with Don Maguire, or Donn na Bin, living there as king of the Fermanagh fairies. When O'Donovan was doing his research for the Ordnance Survey in 1834 he recorded the legend that

"this Donn frequently assisted Maguire in his battles. Tradition preserves one instance of his influence in turning the scale of fight against the English on one occasion at Two Mile River. Maguire exhausted all his ammunition, but by the invisible agency of Donne na Binne, he gained the battle by casting Irish balls (stones)!".[71]

Legends also tell of a giant Horse that would half rise up from Benaghlinn's steep sided peak at samhain-tide (October 31st) and speak oracles, foretelling the future in the following year for people, who would leave offerings up there for him. An older name for the hill is Binn Eachlabhra, the Horse Hill. [22]

Crom Dubh is remembered in this county in many places. Near the village of Belcoo we find Him represented in the form of a solitary standing stone some 2.1m tall, as seen on the left and overleaf. A line carved around the middle of it suggests a rope tying a haystack, which is one of His symbolic forms. The stone calmly exudes power to this day.

Belcoo is on the border with the Irish republic, off the A4 road. Turn west out of this town and at the cross roads at Holywell on the town's edge the small medieval church there has a lovely bullaun stone in the graveyard, surely long predating the church and of pagan import.

Across the road and down some steps, St Patrick's Well, a bubbling spring with a history of healing waters, annual pilgrimage and past Lughnasa celebrations, is a well worth visiting.

The Stone of Crom Cruach is nearby: take the road to Boho from the Holywell crossroads, just past a humpbacked bridge, take the lane on the right past a derelict house; the stone is across three fields after the lane stops.[34]

In County Kildare

Fionn MacCumhaill is often associated with mountain summits, with several called Seefin, Finn's Seat. Fionn, who was cast by MacNeill as a *"degraded version of Lugh"*[22], has a seat on the summit of Almu, the 202m high Hill of Allen, that's surrounded by a sea of bogs. The summit has been inhabited since Neolithic times and it became the seat of the kings of Leinster in the 8th century. Almu was also the name of Fionn's mother as well as a white goddess. A tower was erected on top of his seat in 1859.[16]

In County Mayo

Knockmaa is the premier fairy mountain of the province of Connaught. It's the residence of Finvarra, king of the Connaught fairies, who were said to occasionally fight with the Ulster fairies. (This seems to reflect the memory of centuries of warfare between Ulster and Connaught, following the Iron Age influx into the west coast of Celtic tribes, who then carved out 'sword land' for themselves, pushing the cruithin Ulaid ever to the north-east.[49]) Whoever won the fairy fight would be blessed with the best crops. The Connaught fairies were said to have won in the years 1932 and 1933, as Connaught enjoyed good crops that year. One story of a fairy battle related that:

"two clouds were seen meeting on a certain day (not named) and thousands of midges falling from the sky: it was thought that Finvarra won because there were good crops in Connaught that year." [22]

Knockmaa lies 8km west of Tuam, beside the R333 road towards Headford, just past the village of Belclare. There's a carpark at the base of the hill, near the ruined tower house called Castlehacket. From there, there's a walk of around 30 minutes along a path that winds up to the summit, where the views are far and wide. Four cairns straddle the top of the ridge in a line going east - west. So-called 'Finvarra's Castle' is actually a Neolithic cairn of bleached limestone, with a probable passage grave beneath the huge mound of stones that in the 18th century was re-figured into a folly by the Kirwin landlord vandals.[72] On adjoining hills nearby there are other hilltop cairns.

An interesting take on Fairy Paths, recorded around 1880, relates to Knockmaa. *"The soft breezes that pass one in an evening in West Galway are called fairy paths. They are said to be due to the the flight of a band of the Good People on their way to Knockmaa ... which is their great resort in Connaught. ... A soft hot blast indicates the presence of a good fairy; while a sudden shiver shows that a bad one is near."* [73]

In County Longford

One of the most famous of all the fairy seats of Ireland, Ardagh Hill, south east of Longford town, at 198m high, is the highest point for miles around. The ancient royal centre, home of Midir, is also called Brí Leith. Midir is called a king of the fairies, or the king of the Tuatha Dé Danaan tribe. Some called this the hunting ground of the giant King Midas, a corruption of His earlier name Midir. His Underworld palace is beneath the hill and it was said to have been guarded by three sacred Cranes, indicating an ancient lineage for sure. [23] Midir is immortalised in the 8-9th century story 'The Wooing of Etain' and other classic tales.

It was once a very popular place to go on Bilberry Sunday, the 1st Sunday in August. A flat rock on the summit served as a dancing place. People would report seeing lights hovering near the centre of the summit where there was a swally hole (a crack in the limestone) and youngsters were warned to keep away from it or the giant might grab them and take them in. Through this portal, caves and corridors led to Midir's grand castle in the heart of the hill.

Such was the pagan importance of this site that St Patrick allegedly established an important church close to the hill and it became the parish church. But the Other-world continued to rule the roost there. A quarry on Ardagh hill was said to have been abandoned because people working there were pelted with stones and sods.[34] The Ardagh Heritage and Creativity Centre in the village is very fairy friendly (book ahead for tours and historical events.)

In County Clare

On the western seaboard of Ireland Donn was said to reside in rocky islets off the coast and in coastal sand dunes. Donn's favourite station is beside the sea at Doonaghmore, in sandhills that stretch northwards from Doonbeg (infamous for Donald Trump's golf course). To locals He was a fairy king called Donn na Duimhche (Don of the Sand Dune) and also Donn mac Cromain, son of Croman.

Another source says that He resides in the sandbanks to the west of Ennistymon, by Dough Castle, in an area where Lunaghsa festivities were once celebrated on Garland Sunday. He may be one god, but He has many fractal manifestations.

Local folklore presents Donn as being generally well disposed to local people, helping them if called upon. At night He might be seen riding a white Horse along the sand hills.[22] MacNeill points out that Donn's stronghold around Liscannor Bay is part of a strip of fertile land that stretches inland along the river Dealagh to Kilshanny, and along the Inagh river to Ennistymon. It's the best farmland in the region, so it's not surprising that there are multiple locations for Donn and it reflects the intensive nature of agriculture there from Neolithic times.

In County Cork

Off the Bhéara Peninsula, Donn has a portal to the Underworld at Bull Rock / Tech nDuinn / the House of Donn. The sea rock has a natural archway through it that's considered an entrance to the Land of the Dead. It was the belief that peoples' souls would pass through it in order to enter Donn's domain. An old saying that said, "*to go to the House of Donn*" actually meant that someone was about to die.[74]

In County Kerry

Mount Brandon, on the tip of the Dingle Peninsula, Europe's most westerly point, is the second highest peak in the country, at 953m. It was originally called Slieve Dagdha, the Good God's Mountain. This has long been a sacred mountain of pilgrimage and it's covered with archeological sites; early christians appropriated many of its traditions and replaced the old mountain god with St Brendan. Crom Dubh's home is said to be nearby, at Ballyduff, 4km south east of Cloghane (in Irish Clochan, named for stone 'beehive' huts at the foot of the mountain). The mountain, seen below on the right, is often enshrouded with mist and old Crom would be blamed for any dark, foggy weather.

At the base of the mountain are a couple of small lakes where piast, 'demon serpents', were supposedly confined by St Brendan, as well as at nearby Lough Geal (Chraili), where the back of a female serpent was said to emerge every May Day morning. Place names around the mountain reveal other pagan associations, e.g. the Demon's Cliff, the Hag's Recess and the Bull's Hill.

Lunaghsa festivals once held here were the biggest on the Peninsula. The St Brendan legend said that he converted Crom Dubh to christianity. This was ostensibly the reason for the annual celebration, known as the Patron of Cloghane/ Cloghane Pattern Day, held on the last Sunday in July. It was meant to celebrate the patron saint's day, but actually co-incides with Lughnasa. On that day, originally called the Sunday of Crom Dubh, people would ascend the summit, then do the rounds - praying at a ruined oratory, circumnavigating ancient megaliths and monuments, saying the rosary and drinking from the well. Anyone with a sore back would stand with their back pressed against a pillar stone on the summit, the Stone of the Backs. They then descended the steep eastern path to the village for feasting on the first new Potatoes and mutton pies, and for courtship, dance, song, fun, and games and athletics, such as vaulting over Horses.

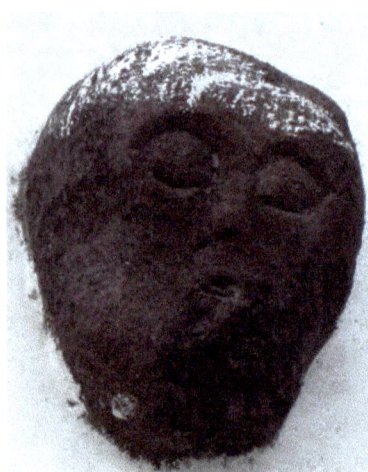

From the gable of a church in Cloghane a lonely carved stone face of Crom Dubh looks down on visitors, the only known representation of him (seen on the left). There has been a revival of the harvest festival there of late. To climb the mountain it's best approached from the west end, along the pilgrim's track, the Saint's Road that begins at the old church of Kilmalkedar, a 9km drive from Dingle. Take the Slea Head Drive (R559) north-west, turn right 1km outside Dingle, signposted An Mhuiríoch, continue for 7km, then turn right at the signpost for Kilmalkedar church.

In County Antrim

The holy mountain Slemish, an extinct volcano some 438m high, east of Ballymena, exudes a powerful presence in the Antrim landscape. Visitors can drive halfway to the top, then take the footpath that circles up to the summit. St Patrick dominates the legends here, but this masks another Other-worldly male presence. Patrick was said to have worked as a slave on the mountain, until angels called him back to Britain. Yet in his own writings he makes no reference to it at all. So we can assume that this was an important pagan place, a fiery power centre.[34]

Original legends appear to have been lost or suppressed. Dowsing remotely indicates to the author that it is the station of a huge male landscape spirit, which would be typical for such a fiery mountain.

Slemish Mountain, Co. Antrim, N.I.

Above - A postcard of Slemish Mountain collected by the author's grandmother when visiting from Australia in the 1960s.

In County Westmeath

Frewin Hill, west of Mullingar, off the R393 and on the road to Bunbrosna, was the traditional home of Eochaidh Aireamh - the Ploughman King. He was said to have taught fairy king Midir, of nearby Ardagh Hill in Co. Longford, how to plough with oxen, suggesting an ancient lineage, perhaps Neolithic. Whether a flesh and blood king, fairy, or demi-god - we can assume a powerful male spirit presence resides here. The summit is accessible, it has Bronze Age barrows and views over Lough Owel. Unfortunately, the hilltop site is spoiled by telecommunication masts.

In County Sligo

A large, but little known and unexcavated mound, 2km south-east of Sligo town is one of a pair on the double hill of Cairns Hill. It's a keynote monument, probably a passage tomb, that features alignments to other hilltop monuments. The west cairn is visible from Knocknarea and Martin Byrne reports that at the time of the equinoxes, if you stand in front of Maeve's Cairn on Knocknarea (please respect the mound and don't climb it!) - the Sun rises over the cairn and

Finding the Mountain Gods

Lough Gill to the west; while if standing on the cairn at the equinox sunset - you can see the Sun setting over Knocknarea.[75] (The east cairn is in the nearby Forest Park. Its alignments are obscured by trees.)

The west mound is traditionally a home of the Daghda. The obscurity of this deity comes from His earthiness, the church couldn't sanitise Him into their own pantheon of holy personalities, so He's been ignored for centuries. But the Daghda still lives here and there, in this case protected by the wildly overgrown, privately owned site. I'm a friend of the caretaker, so I can go there.

Dancing with the Daghda

One full Moon summer's evening a group of women trekked through the site along trails that penetrated thickets of gorse and rainforest regrowth at the ex-farmland site. The women were oblivious to the legend of the Daghda's home, which I'd just discovered in a book[34]. It was a great surprise to find myself taken there and to visit a home of the old god. But when I told the others about Him, it didn't seem to register. Perhaps there was no room for the Divine Masculine in them because they were more focussed on the resurgence of the Divine Feminine. Or had the church achieved its aim?

On that sublime evening at sunset we reached the flat top of Daghda's Mound. Looking out across the hills and sea around Sligo, the glory of Knocknarea lay not far beyond us, while the Ballygawley Mountains, home of the hag goddess, loomed large to the south. The Atlantic Ocean to the west glinted and reflected the setting Sun. The surprising vision of what looked like two Suns over the water was a bonus for our wonderment. We honoured the place, then formed a big circle and drummed and danced freely around.

As I danced the circle, I perceived the arrival of the Daghda, who'd come to check us out. Dark, hairy and animal-like He looked to my mind's eye. He joined in dancing with us, in a wild state of joy and excitement! The memory of past reverences must have been re-kindled in Him. For, even if unconsciously, we were honouring Him by our dancing. I felt His innate goodness radiating out to bless us and was grateful for the privilege of being connected into His presence.

If men could come here to meet the Daghda and strengthen their own Divine Masculine, how great that could be! He is the essence of maleness as a joyful force of benevolence, care, protection and nourishment. But I've just heard that the land is going to be sold. So it's fate is in the proverbial 'lap of the gods'.

Chapter Seven
Finding the Sacred Cow

In the lush green island of Ireland, where cattle rearing has long been the main rural occupation, the Holy Cow is firmly embedded in mythos. She is found across the land, as well as in the sky. Look up into the night sky and you might see the Path of the White Cow, the Milky Way, sprinkling celestial milk as a multitude of stars. The River Boyne, named for the white Cow goddess, was considered a reflection of the Milky Way.

Magical Cows were originally associated with fertility and sovereignty goddesses. Early christian saints Patrick, Brigid and Ciaran of Clonmacnoise then got in on the act and all kept a Cow that gave copious quantities of milk. Ciaran's Cow story is recorded in the 12th century Book of the Dun Cow, the first book in the Irish language. Both Brigid, goddess daughter of the Dagdha, as well as St Brigid, were said to have been reared on the milk of a magic Cow.

There's also the tradition of the Glas Ghoibneann (or Gaibhleann), the magic Cow of blacksmith god Goban Saor (a.k.a. Goibhniu), famous for providing copious quantities of milk to poor people. Her name Glas translates as the grey Cow with bolts of white, but glas also means verdant green, and wherever she grazed the pasture became greener and lusher. While this Cow was associated with the blacksmith god, the original Holy Cow was associated with women and in tradition, only women were allowed to milk Cows and they would spill the first drops of milk on the ground as an offering to the fairies.

As in India, Holy Cow legends were once ubiquitous here. The first Cows in Ireland were said to have magically walked out of the sea, or emerged from inland waterbodies. Many a lake, river, lush green valley and the like have also been associated with magic Cows, who were generous with their milk, but demanded respect. When abused, tricked or subjected to human greed, they would withdraw their bounty. Such tales have deep environmental significance. They function as do Dreaming stories of Australia's Aboriginals, eco-educating people about the necessity for fair sharing of the land's resources, in order for all to live in health and harmony.

Many magic Cow stories have the same theme as the following. A poor family finds a mysterious Cow. No-one knows from whence it comes, nor claims it, so they keep it. The Cow is such a great milker and producer of healthy calves that the family becomes affluent as a consequence. Later on they decide to sell her and the Cow understands this, feels insulted and gathers up her progeny, who all disappear back into her lake or the sea. The family returns to poverty.

In County Donegal

Such stories are found from many areas including Pollen Strand, in the Glenties area and also in Rathmullen on the western shore of Lough Swilly, where a Cow family jumped into the waters to return to the Other-world. Here a rock called Carraig a' Bhaite, at the point of Oilean na nUan, is pockmarked with hollows that were said to have been made by the departing Cow's hoofmarks.[76]

In Counties Meath and Kildare

Boinn, in medieval Irish - Boand, from Bo Fhinn the White Cow, is the premier Irish Cow goddess. The River Boyne in Meath carries her name. Bo is a cow name going back to Vedic India, where it was pronounced Go, as in Govinda. Bo is found in all names bovine. For example, the earliest Irish roads were cattle tracks called bothars.

The traditional source of the Boyne River is located at Trinity Well in Carbery, Kildare, 40km west of Dublin, off the N4 road. Boinn's seat there is in an ancient mound close by and upon which Newbury house sits in old estate parkland, now cattle pasture. Legends speak of nine Hazel trees around the well whose falling nuts bestow special magic into the water. It was believed that by drinking this water in June one could become a poet. A pseudo-legend relates that Boinn disobeyed her husband, water god Neachtain, and tasted the water of this well that was forbidden to Her, causing the waters to rise up and drown Her. The waters flowed out and became the River Boyne. However Boinn is still residing there. It's hard to keep a good goddess down!

The River Blackwater, flowing from Slieve Guaire in Co. Cavan via Kells and Tailtu (the most written about ancient assembly site) and on to Navan where it joins the Boyne, used to be called Guaire's Cow, Bo Guaire. Close to a bend in the River Boyne itself, between Slane and Drogheda, lies the three magnificent passage tombs of around 5,200 years of age, plus associated mounds and megaliths, known as Newgrange, or Brú na Bóinne, the Hostel of the Cow Goddess. Legends overlay legends here and one calls the main mound

Fairy Haunts of Ireland

Aenghus's Hostel, for the son of the union of Daghdha and Boinn. Aengus Óg was fostered by Midir in Brí Leith, but later returned to replace the original goddess and god by trickery. The place is now a major tourist attraction which means having to share Brú na Bóinne with many others when you have your timed visit to go inside the passage tomb. When I visited, I had the impression of a powerful male spirit stationed in the mound.

The great mound was discovered to have significant alignments. Around the days of the mid-winter solstice, sunlight beams in through a roof box above the entrance and down the long stone passageway inside, to illuminate for seventeen minutes the carved back stones in the womb-like corbelled chamber. Probably this was designed to mark time and signify the rebirth of the light half of the year. If you want to view this occurrence you'll have to win the lottery; even then, there may be clouds obscuring the Sun.

> Below - Reconstruction of the main mound has given it a neat look, plastered with pieces of white quartz (considered a magical stone associated with the Sun) that came from the Wicklow Mountains and were found lying around it. Adjacent mounds have also been altered from quarrying and archeological disturbance.

Not far away at the Hill of Tara, the famous royal centre 48km north west of Dublin, the oldest passage grave there, known as the Mound of the Hostages, is a contemporary of Newgrange, i.e. circa 5000 years old. It has its stone passage aligned to the sunrise of November 8th and February 8th (as are Cairns L and U at Loughcrew). While most of the names of the monuments at Tara were conjured up in the imagination of 19th century antiquarians (and the hill's importance overstated), there is a probable Cow goddess connection. Two wells on the hill are associated with Her. The Well of the Calf, on the western side, is in a field where once stood a mound, now vanished, known as the Hill of the Cow. It may have been a passage cairn, which would have attracted the theft of its stones. Its other name was Glas Teamhrach, the enchanted Cow of Goibnui at Tara, who gave Her milk abundantly to one and all.

On the hill's eastern slope is the Well of the White Cow, that was later renamed for St Patrick. Waters flow out of these wells going east and westwards, but they later both join the nearby River Boyne. The February 8th springtime orientation of the passage grave is at the time of the Cow, when the milk of horned animals begins to flow.[34]

In County Leitrim

Like sacred Indian cow Kama-dhenu, the Glas Cow of the Tuatha Dé Danaan could never be milked dry. Glas means green or grey in modern Irish and in this case her name refers to the rich green of lush grass. In the border area of Co.s Leitrim and Cavan a legendary Glas Cow lived around the Glas River, that flows from Sliabh an Iarainn (the Iron Mountain) and on through Miskawn to join the Yellow River at Greaghglas. This Glas Cow grazed along the lush riverbanks at Glangevlin, then continued up across the mountain pass above, wrenching a huge chunk from it as she went, making the gap in the top that is seen today, as in the photo below.[77]

Fairy Haunts of Ireland

Further north in Leitrim, the Glenade Valley has a group of lushly grassed sites associated with a magic red Cow, who could also never be milked dry.

One of Ireland's earliest myths speaks of the arrival of the first Cows to the island, with three sacred Cows emerging from the sea. This 'sea' is probably medieval code for the Other-world, however the first Cows may well have arrived by boat. The black Cow of the emerging trio, Bo Dhubh, turned and headed south. The red Cow, Bo Ruadh, forged off to the north and white Cow Bo Fhinn went eastwards. They went on to beget all the Cows in the land.

These stories must stem from archaic Indo-European roots and I hear a faint echo of Greek myth, where top god Zeus seduced the nun Io, whom he changed into a Cow to avoid his wife Hera finding out. The Cow escaped and went on the run across sea and land. She passed the sea named for her, the Ionian and the first strait she passed was the Bosphorus, beside modern day Istanbul. Bosphorus means the 'Passage of the Cow'. [78]

Sacred Cows pop up in lakes in the River Shannon, literally! Richard Hayward, tells of one such tale. There are two consecutive lakes on the river - Loughs Boderg and Bofin, the Red Cow and White Cow lakes. The story goes that a mermaid in one of the lakes was captured by a local family, who treated her kindly. In return, the grateful mermaid started to tell oracles all around the place. She told the people that if they put her back in the lake on May Eve and if they then gathered on the same spot a year afterwards, she'd give them a hearty blessing in return for their kindness. So they did this.

Sure enough, on the following May Eve, out of the lake waters emerged a splendid pair of Cows, a red and a white one. As the two Cows went their way, they left behind them a fine broad road each, one to the west and one to the east. And that was how those two lakes were named.[30] The same story theme was related by Lady Wilde[79] and pertains to the west coast.

Benbo, the Cow Mountain near Manorhamilton in north Leitrim, towers at 518m high. The place tale describes a man living at the base of Benbo who dreamt three nights running that if he went up to the summit at a certain time then he'd see a Cow emerging from a lake. This small round pond of black bog water never dried up and never flooded out. He was told to stand in-between the emerging Cow and the lake, and that if he spat at the Cow three times, he could possess it. He did this and won the Cow.[80] (This reminds me of being spat on a few times by a Hindu priest in India, as part of a blessing ceremony.)

In County Sligo

In the small coastal port of Mullaghmore, a legendary white Cow would come out of the sea in times of great hunger and head to especially hungry areas, going to Ballintrillik and on to nearby Glenade in Co. Leitrim. She'd make her way to these impoverished townlands where she gave endless quantities of milk, enough for everyone's needs. She returned again and again to do this.

But this ended when a greedy woman tried to milk her dry and keep it just for herself. The Cow returned to the sea at Pollyarry near Mullaghmore and was never seen again.[81]

In County Longford

Near the sacred hill of Brí Leith, about 800m west of the village of Ardagh, the strong stamp of christianity overlaid a more ancient reverence. St Brigid's Well lies at the north east foot of the hill, located three fields off the road, via old double gates. On February 1st, Brigid's Day of Imbolc, people continue to pilgrimage to this well.[82] Nearby was an old convent, perhaps the oldest in Ireland, whose ruins were noted by surveyor O'Donovan as being located on the west side of Ardagh hill.[22]

St Brigid, who was associated with dairying, was supposedly ordained a nun there (and also at other places, allegedly!) She miraculously carried live coals in her dress and where she dropped them the well sprang up.
  "*It is miraculous from that day to this.*
  Cures beyond number are obtained there,"
it was reported of St Brigid's Well in the Schools' Collection of folktales.[83] People would occasionally have visions of Other-worldly nuns alongside a big spotted Cow, walking between the well and the nunnery site.[34]

In County Clare

Situated on the edge of the Burren, Cahercommaun is a massive triple ringed fort with a central stone cashel set high on the edge of an escarpment to the north of the Fergus River, near Caherconnell. This is good cattle country and it was most likely built in the 9th century for the king of North Clare, who would have kept his Cows, received as tribute, safe inside the cashel walls. Legends also say it was the home of blacksmith, Lon Mac Loimtha, which is plausible, as iron working tools were found during archeological excavations there. Lon Mac Loimtha had a magic Cow called Glas Gaibhneach, the Smith's Grey Cow, that was said to be able to fill any vessel. But the smith milked her into a sieve and the copious flow of milk filled the valley, forming seven streams that are still found today below the escarpment.[34]

In County Galway

Located off the west coast, Inishbofin island is named for the white Cow. Legend says that this was once an enchanted island permanently enshrouded by fog. A couple of fishermen got lost in a sea fog and landed on the island, where they lit a fire to dry their clothes. This broke the spell on the island and allowed the fog to lift. Then they watched on as an old woman drove a white Cow down to a lake. On reaching it, the woman struck the Cow with a stick, which turned it into a stone. This angered the fishermen and one of them struck the woman, which caused both of them to turn to stone. To this day, three boulders there are considered to be the petrified white Cow, the old woman and the fisherman.[81]

Finding the Sacred Cow

Above - A statue of Lord Shiva's sacred bull Nandi receives a libation of milk in an ancient temple in Kerala, India.

Chapter Eight
Finding the Cailleach

Finally, in this last chapter we'll look at the greatest of spiritual beings, the primordial Neolithic goddess in Her most powerful form. The Cailleach is the divine hag aspect of the triple goddess, the wise old woman of yore, a shaper and guardian of Country. Many rocks and islands off the south west coast were said to have been made by Her as a giant being and creator of landscapes; while numerous mountains, hills and mounds were formed by stones dropped from Her womb-like apron. As a fierce protector of wilderness and animals, Her personification of wildness carries some degree of legacy from Norse mythology and cosmology.

Constituting all the characteristics of the triple goddess, Her power over fertility and death was invoked by tribal groups who sought Her guardianship. In a later manifestation as the Banshee, She was attached to certain old families. The Cailleach was considered the primordial ancestral being, the *"sovereignty goddess who was appropriated into the political propaganda of competing lineages."* She has been referred to as the *"most tremendous figure in Gaelic myth today"* and *"the most famous old lady in Irish literature."* [84]

Since Neolithic times the Cailleach was invoked in agricultural pursuits and harvest rituals. Great feats, such as Her ability to harvest the corn crop faster than any mortal man, were often attributed to the Cailleach. Into the historical era Her name was used for the last sheath of grain that's either left unharvested, or is ritually cut and plaited, then hung above the harvest feast and kept until sowing time. (Other traditions called this last sheaf Crom Cruach, for the god of harvest.) Sometimes in Co. Sligo the last patch of crop in a corner of the field was not cut at all, but left standing, for the benefit of fairies, the Cailleach and the wild animals it might be harbouring.[81] Environmental wisdom at its best!

Famously known from Co. Cork as Cailleach Bhéara, She has also been called Waura, Beri and Vera; and obliquely referred to as the Red Woman.[85] Her earliest known name was Bui/Boi and, in west Munster, Bui was considered a divine ancestress of the Corcu Loigde, the Tribe of the Calf Goddess, whose king lived at Dunboy/Dun Buithe[86]. She went on to be called in Old Irish Sentainne Berri, the Old Woman of Beare, whose stronghold was based on the Bhéara Peninsula. Another of Her seats is nearby Dursey Island, which is a

Norse name, its Old Irish name being Oilean Bui, and here the island's village is in the Townland of the Cailleach. In the Dinshenchas of Naas, Bui is said to be the wife of Lugh and buried in the mound of Knowth on the Boyne, although that tumulus is millenia older than the story.

The name Bhéara is linked to Bo, the Cow. Bhéara is a derivation of Buvya, the Indo-European for White Cow-like One (in India - Buvinda/Govinda). With the publication in the late 8th or early 9th century of a famous poem, the 'Lament of the Old Woman of Beare', her current name of Cailleach Bhéara became more widespread and it features also in Scottish folk tales. As Aoibheall, the hag goddess of Thomond in north Munster, She was sovereignty queen of the O'Briens, who were the leading lineage there.

The Cailleach not only manifests in Human forms, but also as a bird or serpent, harking back to archaic European goddesses. It comes as no surprise that St Patrick had a penchant for suppressing this great goddess. Medieval scribes delighted in demonising Her as a female serpent/bird fiend.

She suffered banishment, confinement and destruction under the spin-doctor's pens in some forty legends of various locations: at Croagh Patrick (the most well known story) and Downpatrick Head in Mayo (a 35 minute drive northwest from Ballina); at Tullaghan Well in Sligo; at Pulty in Leitrim (a hole below the peak of Slieve an Iarainn into which a stream disappears and where the festival of Lunaghsa was celebrated); at Mam Ean and Tobairin Bhet in Galway; at Lough Derg, Slieve Snaght and Crockalough in Donegal; Altadavin in Tyrone; Slieve Donard in Down; at Teevurcher, Meath (where She was called Garravogue); Lough Derravaragh in Westmeath; Slieve Callan and Kilmacrehy in Clare; Tory Hill in Kilkenny; and in lakes at the base of Mt Brandon in Kerry. Other legends speak of malevolent old women at a host of other sites. Mythic themes of Saints Brigid and Latiaran, who carried burning embers in their apron or skirt from which landscape features sprang, were no doubt based on the creative powers of the Cailleach.

In County Meath

Loughcrew, the Sliabh na Cailli / Hill of the Hag, that's not far from Oldcastle, is the most well known residence of the Cailleach, with its megaliths adorned with beautiful rock art and many legends. The highest part of Co. Meath, it has thirty plus chambered cairns that lie along a ridge of hills and constitute one of Ireland's largest Neolithic cemeteries. It was known locally as The Witch's

Hops and a 15th century reference called it the Three Footsteps of the Hag[87]. Local folk tales say that the Cailleach jumped from one hill to the next, dropping piles of stones from Her apron, a memory of the great goddess, the Divine Feminine, as creator of landscapes.

Like typical passage tombs, the inscribed stone passageways lead into a domed chamber, often with smaller chambers on the sides and sometimes with basin stones where charred human bones have been found. Exposure and weathering of the soft stones have obliterated many of the fine carvings. Most of the cairns are clustered on two hills, Carnbane East, the Sliabh na Cailli and on Carnbane West. The largest and best preserved cairn, on top of Carnbane East and referred to as Cairn T, is traditionally called the Hag's Cairn, or Hag's Cave, as seen below. There has been some 'restoration' and access has been stopped since someone carved their name into a stone recently. Carnbane means white cairn and it was once probably faced with white quartz stones, as these were found scattered around it.

The Hag's Cairn is surrounded by 37 large kerbstones that provided an edge to contain the cairn material. One of these stones on the north end looks rather throne like and it's now known as the Hag's Chair, as seen overleaf.

Finding the Cailleach

Local legends have the Cailleach sitting on it to smoke Her pipe, while visitors also like to sit on it to make a wish, that will then surely come true!

Astronomical alignments mark the spring and autumn equinox times. On those dates, the rising Sun penetrates deep into the central Cairn T, illuminating Sun and other symbols carved on the back stones of the chamber. To the north, Cairn U has alignments to the cross quarter dates of November 8th and February 4th, while Cairn V to the east is aligned to the winter solstice. On the next hill, Carnbane West, Cairn L is aligned to the cross quarter days (as for Cairn U).

From Cairn L was excavated eight round polished stone balls, now in the National Museum in Dublin. Perhaps they represented eggs and the idea of rebirth following death. Pecked hollows in the orthostats (vertical upright stones) are a good fit for these stone balls.[87] Perhaps they were a precursor of the blessing/cursing stones that are occasionally found on stone table altars in old churchyards (and that I've written about in 'Touchstones for Today').

Journey to the Underworld

The full Moon of early August 2023, the harvest month, presided over our women's gathering. It was a 'super Moon', huge for being so close to the Earth. We first each pulled a card from a divination deck. My card was the Spirit of Fire, the element of transformation. But I had no expectations. Each full moon we gathered at each other's homes, where the host organised various spiritual activities.

Next we headed to the nearby Hill of the Hag / Loughcrew and it was a real thrill for me to return to this iconic site. From the car park at the base of the hill we began our evening ascent, first climbing steps that rose up through a tunnel of hedge trees. At the top, emerging into green farm fields, then spiralling around upwards through groups of frolicking sheep to get to the highest point on the ridge.

The sky was getting dark and not far above us clouds blew up and over us. From this highest peak around, the views stretched far and wide. We'd reached the domain of the crone goddess, who created the monuments from an apron full of stones cast down as She bounded across the hilltops.

Finding the Cailleach

We were on top of another world.

To avoid the cool breeze, we hunkered down within the confines of a roofless stone chamber, seen below. It's carved with marvellous symbols and is close to the Hag's Cave. Here we five women cast a ritual circle, honouring the four directions and the still centre. The sacred space created, we shared our inner feelings. Tears flowed as wounds old and new rose to the surface. This special place could help wash them clean, beneath the powerful super Moon.

Drumming began, taking us on a mind journey, a trajectory to who knows where? Rhythmic drumming slows the brainwaves, frees the thinking and imagination for inter-dimensional travel. We followed the shaman's way, the path of our intentions melding with the power of place to influence our experience.

Keen to energetically explore the largest tomb, the nearby Hag's Cave, my mind quickly took me inside of it. I found myself going down, down along its stone passageway and into the corbelled stone chamber at the end. Here stood the mighty Cailleach, proudly stationed in Her ancient stronghold. She greeted

Fairy Haunts of Ireland

me kindly and I briefly bathed in Her awesome power.

Then moving on, I found myself going further, descending down a long staircase to a deeper cave beneath the cairn (not a physical place). There, waiting to greet me, was magnificent Boinn, the white Cow goddess, dressed in a white tunic and crowned with slender upright horns. She stood there sombre and silent. Her priestesses, also dressed in white, were standing around me. I felt comfortable and welcomed, and Boinn told me that my life is following a good path. Then, an unexpected turn of events.

In the deep Under-world cave I found myself standing inside a square fire pit, encircled by the ring of priestesses, with Boinn watching on benevolently in front. Violet coloured flames sprang up, blazed away and totally engulfed me, burning away my flesh. I dissolved in the flames, but it didn't feel bad at all. The Violet Flame is a powerful energy that I'd been invoking in recent meditations as a force for transformation. Before long I'm reduced to just a skeleton of charred bones. I revel in the marvel of the sight of this. There's no sense of fear. I'm just looking calmly down at my burnt black bones with amazement.

When the flames abate, new flesh fills me and I'm re-made and rejuvenated. Unhealthy residues of the past have been burned away. Elated, I thank the beings involved as the drumming starts to slow down to bring us back to ordinary reality. I make my way back up the stairs, go past the mighty Cailleach and return into the physical world. The women remain silent for a while, each reflecting on personal experiences.

Afterwards, at a sharing before closing the circle, it was interesting to hear how some 'personal' experiences were actually part of a wholistic reality. Simone, a professional shaman of thirty years (seen in the photo on page 97), had also met the Cailleach, Boinn and Her priestesses on her own journey. And I got a sense that this site has been used for spiritual initiation and perhaps was a training place for priestesses to work with the Other dimensions. If that's the case, it's still functioning so.

The power of the experience was such that I didn't realise its full significance until the next day. I afterwards felt cleansed and more vibrant than before. It had been such a powerful shamanic journey and connection into the mysteries of the crone goddess!

In County Longford

Corn Hill, a 280m high eminence once called Cairn Hill was a focus for annual pilgrimage on the first Sunday in June. Pilgrims would leave a stone on a cairn there for luck. This could well be an echo of ancient mythos, for the Cailleach was said to have made a cairn on the summit by flying over the hill and dropping stones from Her apron. Archeologists say that the mounds are passage tombs.[22] There's a public walking trail over the hill, but the summit is now spoiled by a large telecommunications mast. To get there take the R198 road from Newtown Forbes on the N4, it's 13.3km to the north east.

In County Armagh

Five miles south of Newry, Slieve Gullion, the highest mountain in the county at 577m, is a volcano that erupted 60 million years ago. It's surrounded by a caldera known as the Ring of Gullion. The Cailleach lives in a deep chamber beneath the huge south cairn on the summit, a passage grave from 3000BC that's locally called Cailleach Birra's House. The entrance is south facing and aligns with Sliabh na Cailleach / Loughcrew some 64km away. Visitors can crawl inside the passage and stand up inside the tall corbelled, octagonal chamber. One legend has Fionn mac Cumhaill being enticed inside the Cailleach's house and later emerging as an old man.[34]

A nearby rocky hillock, The Spellick, is a prominent landmark rich in holy hag mythos. People used to gather there on Blaeberry Sunday for harvest festivities and to pick Bilberries. It also has a special rock known as Cailleach Bhéara's Chair, upon which people take turns to sit on the festival day.[22]

In County Sligo

Sligo is crone country. Here the Cailleach was, in some areas, called Garavogue, or Garvoge, in Irish - An Gharbhog, a name also found elsewhere, that can be translated as 'the rough one'.[88] Perhaps this harks back to Her pre-Neolithic days as a goddess of the wilds. She is credited with building many of the great megalithic monuments in the area, by leaping from summit to summit dropping stones from Her white apron. She is associated with the Hag's Graves, the extensive passage tomb cemetery in Carrowmore; the mounds on the Ballygawley Mountains, a hilly range of gneiss rock that's an extension of

Fairy Haunts of Ireland

the Ox Mountains; and also the massive cairn on nearby Knocknarea, another unexcavated passage tomb that's popularly attributed to Iron Age Queen Maeve, although thousands of years older. [89]

Four of the the Ballygawley Mountains (two are seen below) are topped with cairns. One of these hills is called the Cailleach a' Bhéara and its mound, an unexcavated Neolithic passage tomb that looks like a nipple on a hill breast, is known as Cailleach an Vera's House. From here She was said to have flown out towards Knocknarea to make some animal enclosures with the stones from Her apron. But She accidentally dropped them and this caused the creation of the mounds of the extensive Carrowmore megalithic cemetery.

If you look from the centre of Carrowmore towards the Ballygawley mountains the hills have the appearance of an old woman lying down on Her back. The same view from Cairns Hill west suggests the form of a younger, pregnant woman lying on Her back.

Not far from Carrowmore, Kesh Corann, another of Her hills, commands the landscape south west of Castlebaldwin. Legends about it have a menacing flavour and the power of the Cailleach is very strong here. The large hill is shaped like a hog's back, its steep western side punctuated high up with a line of caves that have long been considered portals to the Underworld.

These caves were home to three fierce hags who, in one legend, fought with Fionn MacCumhail and his Fianna men who were hunting in the area - an invasion of crone territory and violation of Her sacred animals.

Lunasagh festivities used to be held at the hill's base on the last Sunday of each July, known as Crom Dubh's Sunday. High above on the summit is another ancient cairn.[22]

In County Galway

Knockmaa, 8km west of Tuam, beside the R333 road towards Headford, is called Cnoc Mágha in the School Collection stories. Connaught's premier fairy mountain, it's associated not just with the god Finvarra, but also a powerful woman. While medieval stories speak of ancestor Cesair being buried there, it was more anciently considered a place of the Cailleach. A tale collected at adjacent Castlehacket suggests that She was resisting the christian influx, in the form of a Round Tower (that is always part of an ecclesiastical complex).

"There was an old woman who lived on the top of Cnoc Mágha. During her life there was a tower built in Turloughmore. She did not like that so she resolved to knock it. She started to gather stones. It is said that it is she who gathered the large heap of stones on the top of the hill. When she had them gathered she started to fire them. The first one took the roof off it and the second one knocked it to ruins. The men of Turloughmore began to build, but one day as they were building a shower of fire fell from the sky and it burned them all." [90]

From north of Galway city, there's a story about two hills in Poll, grassy hillocks at the far end of the parish of Moycullen. One was topped by a pile of stones. There was a Cailleach living on each hilltop and they had a fight and threw stones at each other. One died from being *"beaten into a pile of bones"*, having run out of stones to throw and She was buried under the pile.[84] It's an explanation for the presence of rocks on a hilltop and shows again the landscape maker at work, in another frenzied show of power.

In County Mayo

North west of Foxford, Cailleach Bhéara lived at the foot of the Nephin ranges, along with Her herd of Cows and Goats.[84] The Nephin hills are made of Precambrian quartzite and cone shaped, so they refract light. They are visible from the R312, Ballina to Castlebar road running between Nephin Man and Nephin Beg ranges.[34]

A tale collected by the Folklore Commission in the 1930s signifies an important mystical site located somewhere in the Nephin hills, that could well be the Cailleach's stronghold. Long ago, the story goes, one Halloween night Paddy Ruadh from Lough Gill in Co. Sligo was feeling uneasy so, as it was a nice moonlight night, he went for a walk. He came up to a local graveyard

Fairy Haunts of Ireland

where he saw a ghost jumping from tree to tree. It jumped down and lifted Paddy over his shoulder and ran away with him, whisking him off in a minute to Nephin Beg in Co. Mayo. The ghost told him that there was going to be a hurling match there that night between the Munster and the Connaught fairies. They waited until the fairies came and the hurling match started. Paddy cheered on the fairies of Connaught and they won the match.

"The ghost gave Paddy a magic pot because he was in favour of the Connaught fairies also. When Paddy went home his wife began to scold him for being away so long. Then Paddy took the pot the ghost gave him and put it on the floor and struck the lid with his fist three times and asked for beef. He took off the lid and there was cooked beef, and they ate a great feed".[91]

This echoes the theme of the generous spiritual being who possesses a cauldron of plenty, for example the Daghda in Ireland, and elsewhere: magic pot wielding goddesses, such as Ceridwen and Rosmerta, and gods Bran and Sucellus.

Croagh Patrick, the conical/pyramid shaped, 762m high mountain of white quartzite, has been the holiest pilgrimage mountain of Ireland for thousands of years. During the Bronze Age there was a settlement around its summit.[92] In historical times it was known as Cruachán Aigle, which probably means Eagle Mountain, and was a major Lughnasa site associated with Crom Dubh and the Caoranach ('devil's mother'), a snake/bird goddess living in nearby Lough na Corra, south of the peak.[22]

According to the pseudo-historical Life of St Colmcille written in 1532, when Saint Patrick banished the 'evil female' spirits from there, they flew off northwards to Glenn Columcille in Donegal. Other myths have it that St Patrick dispelled demon birds by throwing his bell at them and then confining them in Lough na Deamhan, a hollow below the peak. He then faced his greatest enemy the Corra / Caorthannach whom he fought, then confined for a while in Lough na Corra. From there She escaped, flying off to Lough Derg in Donegal, another famous pilgrimage centre.

Around the immediate neighbourhood of Croagh Patrick, the traditional day of pilgrimage was held at the end of July and called the Friday of Crom Dubh, with festivities and love making following afterwards at the foot of the mountain. The modern tradition now is to climb it on the first Sunday in August in a penitential manner, with many walking the rough slopes barefoot,

Finding the Cailleach

and attending a mass held at the summit. Up until the mid 19th century only women were allowed to climb to the top of Croagh Patrick and it was popular with childless women, who'd go there to sleep on the stone bed of the goddess to fructify their loins.[16]

A report from the Swinford area said that "*the older people in the district say the Round Towers were built by Cailleach Bhéara*". In a story of the making of the Meelick Tower, She had wanted it to reach the sky and carried its stones up in Her pockets. But Her plan was thwarted because a boy insulted Her. It was never finished because She then fell off, leaving the impression of Her knees in the rock below.[84] A story of the Round Tower in Balla similarly has a woman as the builder. "*When she had it finished she fell down and she was killed. There are red marks on the outside of the tower. They are supposed to be the spots of the woman's blood*," the informant wrote.[93]

In County Cork

The Cailleach was considered mother of the ancestors of a number of prominent Cork clans, such as the Corca Dhuibhne and Corca Loighdhe. Situated on the Bhéara Peninsula, the Cailleach Bhéara Stone is Her best known representation. This unassuming natural limestone boulder sits overlooking the sea and is said to represent the goddess waiting for the return of Her consort (some say father), sea god Mannanán mac Lir. It's signposted on the peninsula coast road, east of Kilcatherine Point. The stone is bedecked with offerings left by admirers and exudes great charm.

Magan reports on a special sonic association with the stone (seen on the right).

"*People say that Her heartbeat can still be heard from within the stone, though now so slow it's in rhythm with the motion of the waves.*" [2]

Near Fermoy, the Labbacalee / Hag's Bed is the largest wedge cairn in all of Ireland, with huge stones and a most gentle atmosphere, according to Meehan. There are two inner chambers inside triple walls and three huge cap stones, plus some unusual features. A cairn would have once covered it, held in by the ring of kerbstones that remain there.

Within the east chamber the bones of a woman along with bones of Pig, Ox and Sheep were excavated. The woman's skull was placed in the west chamber along with skeletal remains of a man and child. Other human remains were found from later periods.

The Hag's Bed can be accessed off the R512 road north-west of Fermoy, signposted 1.6km south-east of Glanworth.

In County Donegal

Here, the bird/snake goddess Corra/Caoranach is associated with Glencolmcille and most famously at Lough Derg. Pseudo-history has it that St Patrick banished the female demons of Croagh Patrick to various places - to Crew Bay (Mayo), to Tullaghan (Leitrim) and to Glencolmcille, where they stayed until St Colmcille set up his church there. At Lough Derg, the Corra who fled there was allegedly killed by Patrick, although local folklore describe her subsequently rising up in storms and riding the waves.

Christian pilgrims come to do the rounds across the Glencolmcille valley, an area that was more densely populated in Neolithic times. The walk covers 4.8km and pilgrims stop at fifteen stations for prayers and veneration that appears to be a continuation of pagan practises. They visit holy wells, circumnavigate monuments sun-wise, deposit small stones on cairns, lie on a stone 'bed' and, at one station, take a round stone and pass it around their body for healing. Near Station 12 is the Townland of the Demons, where the saint was supposedly attacked by them. West of St Colmcille's Well is the 'Demon's Rock' where Colmcille allegedly banished the demons from Ireland 'forever', meaning that he symbolically gave the goddess the boot, or tried to!

South of Glencolmcille, in the next valley of Malinmore, megalithic monuments abound. About 1.6km from the crossroads and before a shop are located two standing stones and a pile of fallen stones, the probable remains of a dolmen. Known as Cloghacorra, these are the Stones of the Corra.

In County Roscommon

In Lough Key are located three small islets, near where the Upper River Boyle flows into the lake. Buellia is the Irish river name, meaning beautiful female river and in pseudo-history Buellia was the name of the daughter of a king who was drowned when crossing the river, then mourned by the people for nine days. (The number nine could be a clue to signify the old triple goddess, each of Her three aspects having triple forms.)

The three lake islets used to be known as the Hag's Leaps, the legend being that Cailleach na Carraige had leapt from one, called the Rock of Cailleach Carraig, to the others. At each spot where Her feet touched down a tree sprang up, which was said to "*vegetate in full bloom to this day*".[94] Modern place tales from the lake generally ignore this archaic crone connection.

In County Derry

A wedge cairn sitting on a hillside 3.2km east of Dungiven is known as the Cloghnagalla or Hag's Stone (as none of the original covering mound remains). The bones of an adult female were found in a 1938 excavation of the stone chamber and antechamber, as were items of Neolithic age including a polished stone axe, making it a very early example of a wedge cairn. To visit this cairn, turn off the A6 road and go up Boviel Lane for 800m, from where it is visible.

In County Clare

The Cliffs of Moher have a Cailleach connection. The Hag's Head, Ceann Caillí, is a rock formation on the most southerly point of the cliffs. There was once a promontory fort on this head called Mothar or Moher, where now is located the Moher Tower, and the cliffs are named for this fort. A walking path along the cliffs goes past the Hag's Head.

In County Kerry

In an intriguingly archaic folk tale set somewhere in Kerry, the Cailleach of Gleann na mBiorach lived in a cave under a huge rock on the side of a valley.

The name of the glen means the Valley of the Horned Herds, and Deer and Cattle are associated with Her. The Cailleach had lived there since time immemorial, had never changed and never ventured far from the cave. It was a mystery how She sustained herself.

No-one dared to be in Her glen after dark. But one day, before the Sun had risen, an old man was passing through it on his way to feeding his black bull, carrying a sheaf of Oats for it. Looking at the entrance to the cave, he noticed a Heron dropping a big long Eel onto the ground there. Then a white Dog with eight legs appeared from the cave, grabbed the Eel and took it inside.

To his surprise the black bull started to talk to him and told him that the Hag inside had been there since the time of the Fir Bolg (Iron Age, Belgic tribal invaders) and that the Heron was Her mother and the dog Her son. The man and the bull went on to fight the three of them and killed them. Then they went into the cave and retrieved a great treasure of gold and silver pieces.[84]

Legacy of the crone

The treasure of the Cailleach is the wealth of the Earth that sustains us all. As a goddess, She is undying and, as a protector of Country, She deserves our enduring respect. The Earth wisdom of this holy hag can continue to inspire us today if we acknowledge Her sanctity and guard the sacred Earth ourselves. She admonishes us to tread lightly on the planet, to protect the wild places and animals, and to take on board the wisdom of indigenous elders.

May her memory and presence be forever charged with our awe and wonder, kindling great love of the natural world and propelling us into a sustainable future with the fair sharing of nourishment, joy and harmony.

References

1. Personal communication from Wolfgang Kuhl, Germany.

2. Magan, Manchan '32 Words for a Field' , Gill Books, Dublin, 2020.

3. Toibin, Colm 'Lady Gregory's Toothbrush', Lilliput Press, Ireland, 2002.

4. Paracelsus (Philippus von Hohenheim), 'A Book on Nymphs, Sylphs, Pygmies, and Salamanders, and on the Other Spirits', published 1566.

5. Evans-Wenz, W. Y., 'The Fairy Faith in Celtic Countries', Citadel Press Books, 1996, USA (original book 1911).

6. Moore, Alanna, 'Plant Spirit Gardener', Python Press, Ireland, 2016.

7 Yeats, W. B., 'Fairy and Folk Tales of Ireland', Colin Smythe, UK 1973, (originally two books, published in 1888 and 1892).

8. O'Hanlon Rev. John, 'Irish Folklore', E P Publishing, UK, 1973 (original 1870).

9. Deveraux, Paul, 'Fairy Paths in Ireland and Wales - a literature and field study of cognised landscapes in two Celtic countries', International Consciousness Research Laboratories report 2004 - online.

10. Sheldrake, Rupert, 'Science and Spiritual Practices - reconnecting through direct experience', Hodder & Stoughton Ltd, UK, 2017.

11. Giles, Melanie, 'Bog Bodies - face to face with the past', Manchester Uni Press, 2020, UK (Pauli Jensen, 2009 quote)

12. Song at www.geomantica.com/product/wild-in-our-gardens-cd

13 wikipedia

14 French, Claire, 'The Celtic Goddess - great queen or demon witch?', Floris Books, UK, 2001.

15 Wright, Brian, 'Brigid - goddess, druidess & saint,' History Press, 2009, UK.

16 Dames, Michael, 'Mythic Ireland', Thames & Hudson, UK, 1992.

17 Webster, Graham, 'The British Celts and their Gods under Rome', , Batsford Books, UK, 1986.

18 Pattanaik, Devdut, 'Seven Secrets of the Goddess',' Westland Ltd, India, 2014.

References

19 Gimbutas, Marija, 'The Goddesses and Gods of Old Europe 6500 - 3500BC', Thames and Hudson, UK, 1974.

20 Tellinger, Michael, and Heine, Johan, 'Temples of the African Gods', , Makomati Foundation, Zulu Planet Publishers, South Africa, 2009.

21 Evans-Wenz, W. Y., 'The Fairy Faith in Celtic Countries', Citadel Press, USA, 1990 (original 1911).

22. MacNeill, Mairie, 'The Festival of Lughnasa', Oxford, UK, 1962

23 O Tuathail, Lorcan, 'Corr Sceal - Crane Notions', Careful Publications, Donegal, Ireland, 2016.

24 Giles, Melanie, 'Bog Bodies - face to face with the past', Manchester University Press, 2020, UK.

25 Kelly, E. P. 2006. 'Kingship and Sacrifice: Iron Age Bog Bodies and Boundaries', Archaeology Ireland, Heritage Guide no. 35. Bray, Wordwell.

26 O'Donovan, John, 'Ordnance Survey of Ireland: Letters, Cavan and Leitrim, 1836'.

27 www.uisneach.ie

28 wikipedia

29 wikipedia

30 Hayward, Richard, 'Where the River Shannon Flows', Morrison & Gibb Ltd, UK, 1940.

31 McMahon, Joanne and Roberts, Jack, 'The Sheela-Na-Gigs of Ireland and Britain & The Divine Hag of the Christian Celts - An Illustrated Guide', Mercier Press, Dublin, 2001.

32 McGowan, Joe, 'Sligo Folk Tales', History Press, UK, 2015.

33. Magan, Manchan, 'Listen to the Land Speak', Gill Books, Dublin, 2022.

34 Meehan, Cary, 'Sacred Ireland', Gothic Image, UK, 2002.

35 http://www.carrowkeel.com/sites/misc/sheemor.html

36 'Kilclare National School 120th Anniversary 1894 -2014' book.
37 www.duchas.ie

38 O'Flynn, T. N., 'Leitrim Treasure', 1963.

39   Deveraux, Paul, 'Fairy Paths in Ireland and Wales - a literature and field study of cognised landscapes in two Celtic countries', International Consciousness Research Laboratories report 2004 (online).

40   Holiday, F. W., 'Serpents of the Sky, Dragons of the Earth', First Horus House Press, USA, 1973.

41   Moore, Alanna, 'Water Spirits of the World', Python Press, 2012.

42   St Columb's School Moville, Donegal, © The Schools' Collection, Volume 1119, Page 364.

43   wikipedia

44   Webster, Graham, 'The British Celts and their Gods under Rome', Batsford Books, UK, 1986.

45   wikipedia

46   Still Water, a song on the album Wild in Our Gardens. See www.geomantica.com/products/wild-in-our-gardens-cd

47   Healy, Rev. John, 'The Annals of Lough Key' in 'The Irish Monthly', Vol. 6 (1878), pp. 273-283.

48   The Schools Collection, Northyard School, Co. Roscommon, Volume 0253, Page 333. www.duchas.ie

49   O'Connor, Tom, 'Touchstone of Truth, Burden of Pseudo-History', Trafford, 2005.

50   Minto, Susie, 'Leitrim Folk Tales', The History Press, UK, 2013.

51   https://www.rte.ie/archives/2017/0529/878703-lough-derg-monster/

52   https://www.rte.ie/archives/2016/0701/799606-lough-ree-monster/

53   https://www.hinduwebsite.com/hinduism/essays/sacred-animals-of-hinduism.asp

54   Croker, Thomas Crofton, 'Fairy Legends', The Collins Press, 1998.

55   The Schools' Collection, Volume 0161, Page 282 © National Folklore Collection, UCD.)

56   https://visionsofthepastblog.com/2020/10/23/the-madmans-chair-louth-ireland/

References

57 The Schools' Collection, Volume 0516, Page 215 © National Folklore Collection, UCD.

58 The Schools' Collection, Volume 0514, Page 347 © National Folklore Collection, UCD.

59 The Schools' Collection, Volume 0516, Page 216 © National Folklore Collection, UCD.

60 https://voicesfromthedawn.com/city-and-the-paps/

61 wikipedia

62 The Schools' Collection, Volume 0369, Page 677 © National Folklore Collection, UCD.

63 The Schools' Collection, Volume 0369, Page 623 © National Folklore Collection, UCD.

64 https://www.themodernantiquarian.com/site/15430/carrigcleena.html

65 The Schools' Collection, Volume 0369, Page 677 © National Folklore Collection, UCD.

66 wikipedia

67 http://www.megalithicireland.com/Knockmany%20Passage%20Tomb,%20Tyrone.html

68 wikipedia

69 https://uisneach.ie/bealtaine-2021/

70 Mac Coitir, Niall, 'Irish Trees - myths, legends and folklore', Collins Press, Ireland, 2003.

71 Cunningham, John B, editor, 'O'Donovan's Letters from County Fermanagh (1834)', Belleek St Davogs Press, 1993, Ireland.

72 http://www.carrowkeel.com/sites/cong/knockma.html

73 Kinahan, G. H., 'Notes on Irish Folk-Lore' in 'The Folk-Lore Record', Vol. 4, 1881, Published by Taylor & Francis Ltd, pp. 96-125.

74 wikipedia

75 www.carrowkeel.com/sites/coolrea/cairnshill.html

76 Donegal Annual, Journal of the Donegal Historical Society, no 57, 2005
77 Gallogly, Father Dan, 'Sliabh an Iarainn Slopes - history of the town and parish of Ballinamore, Co. Leitrim', Ireland, 1991.

78 Aksit, Ilan, 'The Aegean Mythology - the story of the two sides', Republic of Turkey Ministry of Culture and Tourism Publications, 2010.

79 Wilde, Lady Augusta, 'Ancient Legends, Mystic Charms, and Superstitions of Ireland', published 1888 (available online as a free download).

80 The Schools' Collection, Volume 0195, Page 289 © National Folklore Collection, UCD.

81 McGowan, Joe, 'Echoes of a Savage Land', Mercier Press, Ireland, 2001.

82 http://creativeardagh.blogspot.com/2017/02/st-brigids-day.html

83 The Schools' Collection, Volume 0768, Page 218 © National Folklore Collection, UCD.

84 O Crualaoic, Gearoid, 'Book of the Cailleach', Cork University Press, 2003.

85 http://www.carrowkeel.com/sites/loughcrew/hag.html

86 wikipedia

87 McMann, Jean, 'Loughcrew the Cairns, a Guide', After Hours Books, Oldcastle, Ireland, 1993.

88 Timoney, Martin A., editor, 'Dedicated to Sligo', Publishing Sligo's Past, 2013.

89 www.carrowkeel.com/sites/coolrea/sliabhdaean.html

90 The Schools' Collection, Volume 0025, Page 0075 © National Folklore Collection, UCD.

91 The Schools' Collection, Volume 0155, Page 210 © National Folklore Collection, UCD.

92 https://www.ouririshheritage.org/content/archive/topics/miscellaneous/croagh-patrick-excavations-3

93 The Schools' Collection, Volume 0096, Page 75 © National Folklore Collection, UCD.

94 O'Donovan, John, 'Ordnance Survey Letters Roscommon, 1837', Four Masters Press, Dublin, 2010.

Index

Aeibhill, goddess 66, 94

Áine, goddess, 23, 32, 63, 68, 71, 76

Animism 7

Antrim Co. 82

Athgreany Piper's Stones, Wicklow 39

Ardagh Hill, Longford 72, 79, 90

Armagh Co. 100

Australian Aboriginal lore 5, 12

Balla, Mayo 103

Ballygawley Mountains, Sligo 100

Ballyjamesduff, Cavan 31

Ballymagauran, Cavan 40

Banshee 11, 12, 64, 93

Bealtaine/May Eve 61, 65-66, 70, 76

Belcoo, Fermanagh 77

Benaghlinn, Fermanagh 77

Benbo, Leitrim 89

Benbulben, Sligo 35

Bhéara Peninsula, Cork 80, 104

Bird goddesses 13, 24-26, 94, 105

Blarney Stone, Cork 61

Bog bodies 27, 73

Boinn 52, 86, 99

Brigid, goddess 20, 85

Bui, hag goddess 93

Bull Rock, Cork 80

Cailleach, hag goddess, 24, 29, 45, 93

Caduceus 24

Cairns Hill, Sligo 83-84

Carrowmore, Sligo 100

Caoranach 24, 26, 103, 105

Castlestrange Stone, Roscommon 71-72

Caherconnell, Clare 90

Cahercrovdarrig, Kerry 65

Carberry, Kildare, 52, 86

Cavan Co. 55

Index

Cernunnos, god   21-23

Claddagh Glen, Fermanagh   41

Clare Co.   9, 80, 90, 94, 106

Cleena's Rock, Carraig Clíodhna, Cork   66

Clíodhna/Cleena, goddess   48, 60-61

Cloghane, Kerry   81-82

Clogher Valley, Tyrone   68

Cluricauns   10

Comb, goddess symbol   12, 58, 63

Connemara, Galway   47, 57

Cork Co.   48, 61, 66, 80, 104

Corn Hill, Longford   100

Corra   24, 26, 103, 105

Cullen, Cork   66

Cranes   24- 28, 64, 73, 79

Crane Bag   28, 48

Croagh Patrick, Mayo   32, 102

Crobh Dearg, goddess   65

Croghan Hill, Offaly   73

Crom Dubh, god   28, 29, 77-78, 81

Crow   25

Dagda, god   23, 28, 32, 83-84, 86

Danu, goddess   21, 23, 55

Derry Co.   106

Dingle Peninsula, Kerry   33, 81-82

Donegal Co.   58, 86, 94, 105

Donn, god   23, 28, 41, 44, 75-76, 77, 80

Down Co.   48, 94

Dowsing nature spirits   5

Dunany Point, Louth   60

Dursey Island, Cork   93-94

Dwarf   67

Elves   10

Enniscrone, Sligo   57

Enniskillen, Fermanagh   59

Eochaidh Aireamh, god   83

Ériu, goddess   21, 70

Erne, goddess   21, 58

Etain, goddess   72

116

Fairy Haunts of Ireland

Evans-Wentz, WY 9, 10, 11, 24, 35

Fairy Forts 14

Fairy names 8

Fairy Passes 13, 40, 79

Fairyfield fairy queens 42-43

Fairy wrath 13, 43, 39, 43

Fermanagh 58, 77

Fermoy, Cork 104

Fionn mac Cumhaill 28, 38, 67, 75-76, 78

Finvarra, god 78

Folklore Commission 9, 47, 121

Forest spirits 11

Frewin Hill, Westmeath 83

Galtee Mountains, Tipperary 67

Galway Co. 9, 57, 70, 91, 94, 102

Garavogue, hag goddess 100

'Gentry' 10, 11, 35

Glangevlin, Leitrim 88

Glenade Valley, Leitrim 89

Glencolmcille, Donehal 105

Glenties, Donegal 86

Glentogher, Donegal 58

Gnomes 10

Goddesses and gods 11, 19, 21, 28, 30, 75, 103

Gráinne, goddess 23

Hill of Allen, Kildare 78

Hill of Tara, Meath 87-88

Hill of Uisneach, Westmeath 70

Holy rivers 48

Holywell, Fermanagh 77

Inishowen, Donegal 58

Imbolc/spring festival 20

Inishbofin, Galway 91

Isle of Man 48

Kama-dhenhu 22, 23

Kanturk, Cork 66

Kesh Corann, Sligo 101

Kerry Co. 81, 94, 106

Kildare Co. 20, 78, 86

Index

Kilkenny Co. 94

Killarga, Leitrim 39

Killycluggin, Cavan 31

Kiltoghert, Leitrim 28

Knockmaa, Galway 78, 102

Knocknarea, Sligo 37, 83, 101

Knocknashee, Sligo 37

Knockshegowna, Tipperary 39

Knock Áine, Limerick 64

Knock Firinne, Limerick 75

Knock Grean 64

Lady Gregory 9

Lakshmi, goddess 23

Leitrim Co. 27-28, 37, 88, 94

Leprecauns 10, 39

'Little People' 10

Limerick Co. 63, 75

Longford Co. 72, 79, 90, 100

Lough Corrib, Galway 48

Loughcrew, Meath 94, 97-99

Lough Derg, Donegal 26, 56, 103

Lough Erne, Fermanagh 58

Lough Foyle, Donegal 58

Lough Gill, Sligo 57

Lough Gur, Limerick 24, 32, 63

Lough Key, Roscommon, 53, 106

Lough Ree 56

Loughrea, Galway 48

Louth Co. 33, 60

Lugh, god 28, 29, 30, 78

Lunaghsa/harvest festival 29-32, 39, 53, 58, 60, 66, 68, 76, 78, 81, 100, 101, 103

Maeve, goddess 21, 58

Macha, goddess 69

Mallow, Cork 61

Mannan Castle, Monaghan 59

Mannanán mac Lir 48, 58, 60, 104

Mayo Co. 48, 78, 94, 102

Meath Co. 86, 94

Fairy Haunts of Ireland

Mermaids 47, 51, 56, 57, 71

Midir, god 72, 79, 87

Midsummer festival 64, 100

Monaghan Co. 59

Mount Brandon, Kerry 81

Mount Slemish, Antrim 82

Mullaghmore, Sligo 35, 90

Navan Fort / Emhain Macha, Armagh 69

Nephin Hills, Mayo 102

Newgrange / Brú na Bóinne, Meath 86-87

Northern Ireland 8, 52

Offaly Co. 73

Old Croghan Man 27

Paps of Anu, Kerry 24, 65

Paracelsus 9, 49

'People of Peace' 10

Pilgrimage 16, 17, 20, 32, 35

Quantum physics 7

Rathmullen, Donegal 86

Red Woman, hag goddess 93

River Bann, NI 52

River Blackwater 86

River Boyle 53

River Boyne 52, 85

River Shannon 55, 76, 89

River Slaney 52

Rock of Cashel, Tipperary 67

Ross Carbery, Cork 60

Roscommon 48, 53, 71, 106

Sacred Cow 60, 85-92

Samhain/Halloween 36, 74, 76-77

Shannon Pot, Cavan 55-56

Sheela-na-Gig 33, 45, 67

Sheemore, Leitrim 37 - 39

Shiva, god 21, 22, 29, 30

Silvermines Mtns, Tipperary 67

Slieve Gullion, Armagh 100

Sligo Co. 12, 35, 57, 90, 94, 100

Slievenamon/Hill of the Women, Tipperary 67

Index

St Barry's Well, Roscommon 53

St Brigid 19, 74, 85, 90, 94

St Colmcille/Columba 26

Swinford, Mayo 103

The Spellick, Armagh 100

Tipperary Co. 39, 67

Tir Na Og 12, 63

Toghers (bog trackways) 27

Totemism 24

Triple deities 20-21, 28, 65-66, 93

Tuatha Dé Danaan 21, 23, 30, 70

Turoe Stone, Galway 70-71

Tyrone Co. 68, 94

Uisneach, Westmeath 29

War goddesses 20, 26

Water fairies 47

Water-Horses 47

Westmeath Co. 70, 83, 94

Wexford Co. 52

Wicklow Co, 39

Yeats, W.B. 9, 12, 35

Resources

Irish Diviners Association -
Membership includes talks and excursions.
Contact - **irishdiviners@yahoo.ie**

Folklore Commission
Recently digitised folklore from many parts of Ireland, including stories collected by school children in the 1930s.
www.duchas.ie

Mythic Mountain Tours
Inviting you to visit magical and sacred sites of north-west Ireland, including one thousand year old Round Towers, Neolithic monuments, holy hills and wells, goddess mounds, fairy places, etc.

Alanna Moore will guide you in how to experience the Other-worldiness of these special sites, attuning to places "where the veils are thin".

Customised, or 'magical mystery' tours for small, self driving groups of four to twelve people.

Accomodation in a low electro-smog house, dowsing/geomancy tuition and garden produce for self-catering are available.

Request a quote. Organise your group and book an unforgettable trip for next summer or autumn. A limited number of dates between April and September are available.

See **www.geomantica.com/events/mythic-mtn-tours/**

Dowsing Services
Do you sleep in a healthy place?
Could there be a sacred site in your backyard?
Where do the local nature spirits reside and are they happy?

Find out with a geomantic survey by Alanna Moore.
House and land surveys available by remote map dowsing to identify areas of disturbed or beneficial energy and nature spirits.

See: **www.geomantica.com/product/geomancy-consultancy-by-map-dowsing/**

Resources

Books by Alanna Moore
Available from www.geomantica.com

Divining Earth Spirit
- an exploration of Global and Australasian Geomancy

1994, 2nd edition 2004.
ISBN: 0646217003
232 B5 pages

The Earth is alive, conscious, sacred and pulsing with vital forces! Subtle energetic and spiritual dimensions of the environment and our sacred relationship with it, from Aboriginal and Maori traditions, through to the ideas and work of modern Earth mystery researchers and dowsers globally. With an Australasian bias, it has relevance for Earth stewards everywhere. Includes a global geomantic overview, the problem of geopathic stress, aspects of Earth energy dowsing, sacred site awareness, the devic dimensions and the consciousness of landscape; with several geomancers contributing their own personal insights into geobiology and the spirit of place.

Touchstones for Today
- designing for Earth harmony with stone arrangements

2013. 142 A5 pages. ISBN: 978-0-9757782-5-8

Ancient standing stones can transmit beneficial Earth energies and provide anchor points for the power and spirit of the land. Old traditions of healing, divination, wish fulfillment and fertility associated with certain stones continue to hold currency today. Many are portals for the Earth/Sky/Other Worlds and inner connection. From Britain's Stonehenge and stone altars in Ireland, to Aboriginal people's stone arrangements with cosmological connections in Australia, to modern labyrinth making - the urge to work with stones spans the world. Discover the potential today to bring greater harmony to the land using stone arrangements. Find out how to design and make your own stone circles and labyrinths, for enhanced backyard feng shui. A practical guide.

Water Spirits of the World
- from nymphs to nixies, serpents to sirens

2012. 144 A5 pages.
ISBN - 978-0-9757782-4-1

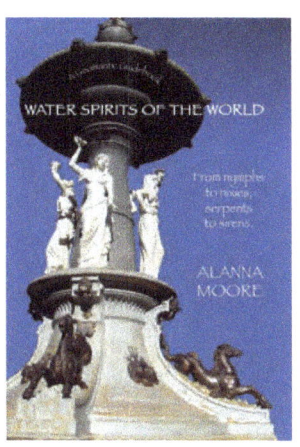

Opening windows onto the genius loci of watery landscapes, this book brings alive a rich tapestry of ancient geo-mythos. From the Otherdimensional reality of Australia's Aboriginal Dreamtime to the modern art of dowsing the devas, this book will delight and surprise. For seekers of the soul of landscape, it provides unique insights into the spiritual nature of life and sacred watery places.

The author is a master dowser inspired by the nature spirits to care for and love the sacred Earth.

Plant Spirit Gardener

2016. 206 A5 pages, all colour photos.
ISBN: 978-0-9757782-9-6

Gardening can deeply nurture our heart and soul, especially if we are aware of the invisible realms and become a co-creator with the spirits of nature. With the down-to-earth esoteric wisdom in this book we can practise Divine Gardening. As well as ancient folklore, there are scientific insights and descriptions from modern day clairvoyants and dowsers to illuminate the spiritual realities of life and landscape. All a sensitive gardener needs to profoundly connect with Mother Nature is here. There are instructions for learning pendulum dowsing for the garden; how to experience the Otherdimensional worlds; and ways to energetically enhance the environment.

With the suggested exercises and applying dowsing to the summaries, charts and lists provided, honing the intuitive faculties is made easy. This unique reference book is richly illustrated to help you learn the fascinating art of gardening with the devas.

Sensitive Permaculture
- cultivating the way of the sacred Earth

2009. 136 A5 pages
ISBN: 978-0-9757782-2-7

Drawing upon indigenous wisdom, this book explores the living energies of the land and how to connect with them via gardening. It combines insights of geomancy and geobiology with eco-smart Permaculture design, offering an exciting new paradigm for sustainable living. (The author has three diplomas in Permaculture from originator Bill Mollison.) Brimming with practical tips for eco-spiritual gardeners, it encourages us to live sustainably in harmonious co-operation with nature and to practise sacred custodianship of Country.

The Wisdom of Water

2007. 250 A5 pages
ISBN – 978-0-9757782-1-0

Fresh water tends to foul and vanish when human impacts are high. But we can reverse the trend and re-connect with the wisdom and healing powers of water. And there's plenty of New Water to tap into to, if you know how to look for it - by dowsing. In this book Alanna delves into water's mysterious origins and manifestations, its energetic and spiritual aspects, global traditions, plus water in Australasian landscapes. It gives holistic understandings about water from a geomancer's perspective, including water divining, historical, esoteric and indigenous perspectives.

About Alanna Moore

The author, from Sydney, Australia and now living in Ireland, has an Irish/English heritage and thus an appreciation of fairies comes naturally to her. Her mother would often blame mishaps on 'the pixies' and they made useful scapegoats. She inherited the good intuition of the Irish and it has kept her safe and sound.

A professional geomancer / dowser for over 40 years now, Alanna has devoted her life to raising the profile of dowsing and sharing its great potential by teaching and writing about it. She was a founder of the New South Wales Dowsing Society, based in Sydney, in 1984 and has been a speaker at various dowsing society events internationally.

This is Alanna's tenth book and it encapsulates a lifetime of experiences with the Other worlds.

Alanna has also made 21 documentary style films on geomantic subjects and has recorded two albums of original songs, available on CD.

These are available at her website, as well as the stone pendulums she makes, plus related products, as well as loads of information.

www.geomantica.com

www.ingramcontent.com/pod-product-compliance
Lightning Source LLC
Chambersburg PA
CBHW062051290426
44109CB00027B/2794